Collected Poems
1986–20(

CH00919599

GREG DELANTY was born in Cor
lived in Cork until 1986. He no
Vermont where he teaches at S....
three months of each year he returns to his Irish home in
Derrynane, County Kerry. Delanty has received numerous
awards for his poetry, including the Patrick Kavanagh Award
(1983), the Allan Dowling Poetry Fellowship (1986), and the
Austin Clarke Centenary Poetry Award (1997). In 1999 he
was a prizewinner in the National Poetry Competition. He
has received an Irish Arts Council Bursary, and has been
widely anthologised. He is politically active and ran for the
Vermont Green Party in the US elections.

Also by Greg Delanty

Poetry Collections
Cast in the Fire
Southward
American Wake
The Hellbox
The Blind Stitch
The Ship of Birth

Special Poetry Editions
The Fifth Province
Striped Ink

Translations
Aristophanes, *The Suits* (originally *The Knights*)
Euripides, *Orestes*
Selected Poems of Kyriakos Charalambides

Anthologies
Jumping Off Shadows: Selected Contemporary Irish Poets
(with Nuala Ní Dhomhnaill)
The Selected Poems of Patrick Galvin
(with Robert Welch)

GREG DELANTY

Collected Poems
1986–2006

CARCANET

First published in Great Britain in 2006 by
Carcanet Press Limited
Alliance House
Cross Street
Manchester M2 7AQ

Reprinted 2007

A CIP catalogue record for this book is available from the British Library
ISBN 1 903039 82 7 (pb)   ISBN 1 903039 83 5 (hb)
978 1 903039 82 3   978 1 903039 83 0

The publisher acknowledges financial assistance from Arts Council England

Typeset in Monotype Janson by XL Publishing Services, Tiverton
Printed and bound in England by SRP Ltd, Exeter

Introductory Note

These are the poems I want to keep in print, collected from over twenty years. I have not included every poem from each individual collection, and I have altered some poems from their original book publication. Since a number of poems from *Cast in the Fire* (1986) appeared in my second book, *Southward* (1992), and because these two books have approximately the same register, I have included both books in one section. The four poems 'To Belarussians after Chernobyl', 'The No-Go Land', 'Live' and 'Janus' were included in Adi Roche's book *Children of Chernobyl* (1996). *The Fifth Province* was a special edition mostly made up of poems from *American Wake*, except for the two included here, 'Spiritus Hiberniae' and 'Film Directions for the Underworld'. *Aceldama* is published here as a collection for the first time.

Greg Delanty
January 2006

Acknowledgements

Poems from the unpublished collection *Aceldama* have appeared in *Agenda, Cúirt Annual 2005, The Green Mountain Review, The Irish Times, Poetry Ireland Review, The Southern Review, Southward* and *turnrow*. I would like to thank their editors and the editors of newspapers, journals, magazines and anthologies who first published poems from previous collections, as well as the editors and publishers of those collections.

The following poems were first published in *The Atlantic Monthly*: 'Loosestrife' (November 2005), 'The Bindi Mirror' (January 2001), 'Tagging the Stealer' (June 1997), 'The Compositor' (August 1995) and 'After Viewing *The Bowling Match at Castlemary, Cloyne, 1847*' (February 1995).

For more detailed explanations of slang words than I have given in the Notes, see Terence Patrick Dolan's *A Dictionary of Hiberno-English: The Irish Use of English* (Dublin: Gill & Macmillan, 1999), Bernard Share's *Slanguage: A Dictionary of Irish Slang* (Dublin: Gill & Macmillan, 1997), Seán Beecher's *A Dictionary of Cork Slang* (Cork: Goldy Angel Press, 1983), and the web site www.hiberno-english.com.

For *The Hellbox* I consulted Joseph Moxon's *Mechanick Exercises on the Whole Art of Printing*, as well as general printing handbooks.

The epigraph of 'The Leper and Civil Disobedience' is from Seán Connolly, *Journal of the Royal Society of Antiquaries of Ireland* 119 (1989).

Contents

The Ship of Birth (2003)

News in Flight

We fly over the city. The screen flashes current news.
  Nothing it seems but killing and mayhem all round.
Daily we're brought low, how lowly we've fallen.
  Hardly anyone says a word. Urban lights stretch into
the rural night below. Even fewer mention such wonders.
  The lights are like those of countless fans at a concert
holding up candles to their gods, the group Homo sapiens,
  fleeting as any. Yet gods nonetheless,
bearing mayhem on the one hand and marvels
  on the other, as is the way of any regular band of gods.

Gregory of Corkus
from *The Greek Anthology, Book XVII*

Cast in the Fire
(1986)

and

Southward
(1992)

Preludes

I
First Date

Strolling his beat,
A Saturday-afternoon street,
Blessed & braided with girls,
His eyes hoard a girl in a brown veil of sunlit hair,
Marking her not from one to ten,
But from ten to infinity.
His heart tittuping to the click of her approaching heels.
Both pretend to be discreet.
Both prepare to meet.

II
Just Married

His flashing ring answers hers
Like the reflecting mirrors of prisoners,
Signalling from one wing of cells to another,
Speaking a language of light,
Planning their escape for that night.

Skin-head pigeons strut in a gang
Along the road's white line
And fly from under a fuming cop car.
Lazy, contented seagulls catch rides
On the conveyor belt of a river.
Others glide & hover in the slow air
Of a busking tin-whistle player
As if conjured from his upside-down hat.
Singing thrushes play on the fret board
Of electric wires, and sparrows
Arrow upwards, seemingly desperate
To enter heaven, not noticing heaven
Has descended to the ordinary
As we saunter along Union Quay.

You're sure you heard something break, something snap
Within her. Like a twig split in two
And cast in the fire. Or like the snap
Of a violin string, halting all music.
Witnessing tears break in her face
You discovered the magic, the black magic
Of your words, no magic could take back.
You shattered a vase of flowers and fled
As if from yourself out into the dark.
Leaving her to pick up the flowers,
Restring the violin, await your next attack,
But this time of fawning words & flowers,
And her breakfast in bed for at least a week.

Though it has never happened, you know
How it feels to fall overboard at night;
To discover your cries go unheard by the crew,
Drowned out by the wind, sea and boat.
You're almost sure someone pushed you,
Though maybe you threw yourself over,
Or could you have fallen accidentally?
It feels like all three. It's not icy water
That petrifies you, but the depth of sea,
Full of prehistoric creatures closing in
On you as you helplessly tread waves,
And the darkness sucking you under.
It is not water you tread, but darkness.
The dreaded creatures baiting you are in you.

Below 'The Devil's Punchbowl'

It was a pagan place, the waterfall:
A giddy stream leapfrogging
Nymphs with long silver hair.

You knelt, not sure why you should kneel,
As if in supplication, bathing
Your hands & face before drinking –

Scared later when informed
That 'the cloven-hoofed chap drinks
From the same waters upstream';

Shades of the fear, a thrill
Almost, after drinking from the source
Of each babbling poem you write.

You ignore the perpetual *shhh*
Of the fall with its white finger to its lips.

It is like the way breath is taken
When you plunge into icy water –
And, at the same time, like the sting
Of a jellyfish, camouflaged by water,
Catching you around your caged heart –
Discovering her body is so coral fragile;
Her nipples, limpet shells, cling to her bikini.
You sense something even more fragile
Within her that has naught to do
With the make-up of body tissue.
And like mussel shells open to high tide,
Laced to rock, something opens in you,
Strengthening love's byssus. As seagulls
Clap, the wave's frilly curtain falls.

Below Zero

About the time she turned from him
A strange bird was sighted
Throughout the outskirts of the city:

The Mohican-headed lapwing
Driven by the cold
Out of its ice-bound meadow –

Just like her coldness drove him,
Trembling, from the habitat
He had long taken for granted.

And though the sun has thawed
The lapwing's meadow, he still wanders
In a silence below zero.

Dawn

Though you're standing, there's something kneeling
Within you, beneath a wafer-like sun,
Raised in the red-raw hands of morning,
Hypnotised by the sky's rose chasuble,
The mist's wandering incense
And the decked-out altars
Of fishing trawlers.

You take the pale host from pink fingers,
Letting it melt from a dry palate.
A dove-like gull descends, flying low,
Smoothing out the sea's white lace.
You bow, seeing the host go
Behind a dark cloud's arras,
And turn in the risen sun's glow.

A Common Story

I think had anyone come upon us
They would have noted how the shades
Of lovers hesitantly walked arm in arm
Up a desolate, tree-tunnelled street.
We held each other as if we'd just met,
Rather than a couple about to part.
You wept and there was guilt in your tears
For you, more than I, were the one leaving.
Knowing loss would spur me to lament
You entreated, 'Sing the happy days as well.'
But now, years later, as I attempt to,
I looked back and you are Eurydice
Struggling down a dark endless street.
Neither of us can do anything to turn you.

Tie

Without asking, you borrowed your father's black tie,
Sure he had another black tie to wear
Should some acquaintance or relation die.
But had he? He should be here somewhere.
But where? Could he be at home on this dark day,
Ransacking drawer after drawer for a funeral tie?
Yes, that must be what has kept him away.
Though you are sure you saw him, tieless,
Smiling over at you, before you lost him again
Among the keening cortège. Leaving you clueless
To his whereabouts, till earth, splattering a coffin,
– or was it the wind ululating in each prayer? –
Informed you that you can never give your father
Back his black tie, though you'll find him everywhere.

Interrogative

Even the flimsiest, most vulnerable creatures
Are equipped with devices to outwit death:
The night moth blends into its surroundings,
Lichen-coloured, it conceals itself on bark;
Other creatures don the colours of a wasp,
Fooling predators into believing they can sting;
But how could your father outwit death's grasp,
Snatched forever & too soon, under its dark wing,
Always out in the open without sting or cunning?

Leavetaking

After you board the train, you sit & wait,
  To begin your first real journey alone.
You read to avoid the window's awkwardness,
  Knowing he's anxious to catch your eye,
    Loitering out in never-ending rain,
To wave, a bit shy, another final goodbye;
You are afraid of having to wave too soon.

And for a moment you think it's the train
  Next to you has begun, but it is yours,
And your face, pressed to the window pane,
  Is distorted & numbed by the icy glass,
    Pinning your eyes upon your father,
As he cranes to defy your disappearing train.
Both of you waving, eternally, to each other.

At three in the afternoon
a light is on.
I am watching rain
congregate & weep
on a windowpane.
I am back in another room
anxiously waiting
to be nine.
You won't allow me out
in bad weather to play.
You and a framed pope
are turned away.
Christ's eyes forgive me
wherever I stray.
I want you to tell me
of wondrous deeds,
but you count links
of rosary beads
or count stitches,
knitting Norman sky-blue britches.
I can't quite remember.
You order me
to leave him sleep
in the pen.
I badly want
to climb in then.
Instead, I squeeze my hand
through the bars
and take his baby hand
in my boy's hand.
He stirs,
but does not wake.

Then for no apparent reason
I cry
quietly,
not wanting you to see
more than I want.
The hours go by.
Flames flick
through the slack
holding the blaze back
until the return of your spouse
at a quarter past five sharp
into your wipe-your-feet house.
You allow me out
to open the gate
so he can drive straight in.
I am afraid
of the dark.
I've always been afraid
of the dark.
In the kitchen
you keep one eye
on the kettle.
Mother, a watched pot
never boils. Remember?
Norman has just woken
and starts to cry.
He wants one of us to lift him
into the sky.
I stand listening
for our car
at the open gate.
Your husband, our father,
is late.

The Master Printer

Though it's May, it is the first spring day.
You are giving me a crossbar to school.
I'm wondering will Adolina Davy or Lily Walsh
notice me in my first long pants.
We weave through fuming, hooting cars,
outwitting lunchtime traffic.
Our new front wheel is answering the sun.

You inquire am I okay.
I confide my behind's a bit sore.
You laugh, say we haven't far to go.
But I never want to get there.
We wave each other off. I run pell-mell
to buy a pennyworth of Bull's Eyes,
escaping the thought of the line-up bell.

I hide the sweets beneath my inkwell.
My nothing-to-hide look reveals them
to the all-seeing eyes of Brother Dermot.
He smiles, orders me to put out one hand
and then the other, caning until
both my palms are stinging pulps,
as he has beaten so many, so often,

distorting each palm's destiny.
Did that brother harm you too,
summoning you in to declare
that I, your son, was a *bit* slow?
He did not know, blind behind a frown,
that you had the master printer's skill
of being able to read backwards & upside down.

17

Setting the Type

I pick a magnifying glass from your desk
and hold it to a haze of men
bowed over the jigsaw puzzles of galley trays.

You confer with Dan Hannigan.
I wonder at the results of a half-century
of nicotine on his right index finger.

Through zig-zag bars of an old-fashioned elevator
I have just spotted the ascending head
and Humpty-Dumpty body of Donnie Conroy.

He will be broken by drink
and his daughter's death.
Her face is now smiling from his desk.

You turn and escort me to the letterpress.
Mr Lane punches my name into shiny lead
and declares hereafter it is eternal.

The names of Dan Hannigan, Owen Lane, Donnie Conroy –
I could go on forever invoking the dead –
were set deep in a boy

impressed by the common raised type on the 3rd floor
of Eagle Printing Company, 15 Oliver Plunkett Street,
in the summer-still, ticking heart of Cork City.

The Emigrant's Apology

to my mother

As you led us single-file up the main aisle
I prayed you wouldn't pick a front pew,
aware you wanted to be as close as possible
to God and show off your latest hat too.
It wasn't just that I didn't want people
thinking I was religious, but that I knew
my devotion would be threatened by a conspiracy
of giggles no later than the sermon,
unable to take any sort of solemnity.
My strategy, once I felt them coming on,
was to conjure horrors: homework I had to do
but couldn't, a toothache, a spoon of medicine.
Now all I would have to think of is you
wearing a black scarf alone in a front pew.

Complaint to the Watchmaker

to my parents

You gave me a watch for First Communion,
but I couldn't get the knack of reading
which was the hour and which the minute hand.
Watchless boys surrounded me
like the numbers around the arrows
and cuckooed the confusing time.
Sister Benedict asked *an t-am* daily,
knowing I'd end up guessing or dumb
while the crucifix pendulum swung
over her unthinkable thighs and I prayed
the hour hand would turn into the second.
Years turn into minutes. You are gone.
I'm like that watch that needs shaking
each morning to set the hands ticking on.

The Brothers

The night you got transferred from the jail
of your cot to my low-security double bed
we drew an imaginary line down the middle.
Should either trespass the other's side,
he could pound the offending party.

Being older, I had the advantage,
as you discovered earlier, following me
while I played cops & robbers with boys my age.
You slowed me up, got me shot so often,
I spent most of the time playing dead.

We were partners on kitchen raids,
sharing spoils undercover with a flashlight.
Now after a shindy we both play dead,
grapple for words to bring us back to life
out of the reserve stashed for the needy night.

The Rising

for Terence Brown

We struggled to stifle giggles as Brother William
recited for the umpteenth time *Dark Rosaleen*.

But even more hilarious than his shut-eyed fervour
was that he insisted Ireland was a queen.

Though whenever we had to draw it freehand,
he had us imagine the profiled head of a man:

below the receding blond hair of Northern Ireland
was Monaghan's ear & Lough Erin's weeping eye;

Clare's moustache drooped beneath the nose of Galway,
over the Shannon's mouth to join Munster's beard;

the severed head talked rigmarole with the USA
and was turned from that perpetual bully England.

It was worth three on each hand for raising our arms
out of devilment and declaring it was just land.

Home from Home

Perhaps now I understand the meaning of home
for I'm in a place, but it is not in me
and could you zip me open you'd see,
between the odd break in fuming clouds,
an island shaped like a Viking's bearded head,
gasping & floundering in the invading sea,
with its crown crookedly stitched,
looking as though it will never heal.
Then zoom below the most vulnerable spot,
dictating all at the back of this unruly head,

to a city in the Adam's Apple
and we'll rollercoast down Blarney Street
to Shandon Steeple launching into the sky,
propelled by its Salmon of Knowledge vane.
We'll sightsee the town's heart to grey, squat City Hall
wearing a green zucchetto on its clock-faced tower.
We'll avoid eyesores, the odd mean-spirited native,
and end up in some pub with you bothered
by the rapid slagging & knawvshawling that are
loaded with words you'll find in no dictionary.

Their confab will be heated as if by the Gulf Stream
and the Mediterranean sailors docking there.
As talk continually dips & rises,
like the lilting hills surrounding the city,
you'll think they're about to break into song,
but there'll be no singing till the ritual egging on.
I'll introduce you to all & sundry,
even to those who are dead & gone,
or just gone, unable to make home at home.
When time is called, we'll stagger from this poem.

23

The Unknown Citizens

particularly for the Simon Community & Joe Byrne

Different-coloured balloons
drift
from a packed bunch
on a crowded avenue.

Nobody,
not even the balloon-seller,
notices them disappear
into the blue.

The Fable of Swans

to Adi Roche and CND

I can't quite recall
how my dream went.
You're floating lanterns
down the Lee.
We stop to see,
and realise you're giving
some sort of gift.
A swan sails by,
its neck a question-mark.
Someone asks is it freedom
from the dread
of something shaped
like a common fungus
blooming
in some general's head?
As you nod,
the swan unfurls its neck
and takes off
down the river's runway,
clearing other swans
with heads
ostrich-buried
in murky water.

The Lizard & The Lover

Do you remember the lizard
we saw basking on a rock
in tropical Derrynane?
Repulsed, your hand
tightened in mine.

Today in Miramar,
on spotting a salamander
laze in parched grass,
I realised you are repelled now
by my relentless wooing.
Your hand tightens
in another's.

Two for Joy

During the night a heavy fall of rain
cleared the air. We can breathe once more.
The sun cools itself on the ocean
that lackadaisically defines the shore.

The shadows of a school of whale-grey clouds,
sweeping the sea's surface, bamboozle
fish into thinking that leviathans glide
overhead and send petrified shoals

ducking for cover in every direction.
The giants beach themselves on Eagle Hill.
Cormorants perch on a rock off Carrigbreakan
with open wings welcoming the wind.

Two white butterflies use it
to raddle through air before they land
for fuelling on nodding Forget-Me-Not
and then bask on a heart-shaped leaf.

I wish I could tell them they've no need
to brandish false eyes to scare me off.
And maybe somehow they understand
since they close them and *ceilidh* toward me.

A tourist frantically waving a bee away
is conducting the climax of a symphony.
Another wants to snapshot the soul of the bay.
Two magpies scuffle, all cacophony.

They vie for a partner who seems coy.
These stroppy, sozzled graduates in tuxedos
cop she's long gone with another boy
and flap off, the best of buddies.

An Oil Spillage

A highdiving gannet opens any point
in the water and a circle radiates out,
verifying that every point is the centre.

Tern scissor the gauze of the heat haze,
snipping the air from Africa, and nest
under the sky's sunset fuchsia blaze.

Kids cart a dinghy overhead
and reverse from a crab retreating from them
as if the film was held and run backward.

Bull Rock seems ready to charge out
to sea head down, away from danger
rather than on the attack.

None can escape the dark spreading here.

The Scarecrow

Since the tide is in, we walk the roadway
bordered by fuchsia & honeysuckle.
Cairns of turf & hay ring Cahernageeha
like sacrifices for a fine day.
Dark clouds veil its peak as if concealing
Celtic gods disputing the offerings.
A hare kangaroos out of the bush
and vanishes up a burrow's sleeve.
Ogham letters are like notches cut by
an inmate dreaming of freedom & a woman.
You charge that you'd be better off
talking with the nearby scarecrow.
If you must know, I was thinking
that, until we met, I was the prisoner.

The Worrier

That night we drove from Valentia,
   the fog curbed hurry,
not to mind my daily bout of worry
   as the car fretted over Coomakista.

To divert me from the edge of doom
   after we near plunged over the head,
you said cats' eyes were the bread
   Hansel scattered through the gloom.

Tonight, making my way on my own,
   a murder of crows picked off my trail.
I pulled by the roadside to phone,
   enticed again into the hag's jail.

I need you to outwit that witch of worry,
   worrying now you're tired of my worry.

On Returning

I promised an orange plant from Florida
but by the time the bus reached Virginia
I doubted it could survive the cold
and prowled beneath seats for hot air,
afraid you'd take it as a portent
for rootlings spreading between us,
tentatively and unseen, should it die.
Three years later it still flourishes,
keeps tropic time in our front window,
growing most when outside is cloaked
in snow like the sheet-covered furniture
of a summer home abandoned for winter.
Since we're apart a snowstorm's blown, but
soon we'll admire how our plant has grown.

A Wake on Lake Champlain

As an F-16 unzips the sky
a white-sailed yacht races in
like a surrendering rider
from the plain of the lake and a boy
conjures doves with a piece of cake.

Gas pumps plug their fingers in their ears.
You can hardly hear a child start to cry.
Her father fails to rock her still.
Afterwards he remarks that this jet guards
Plattsburgh Nuclear Base or is on border drill.

Now she's mesmerised by a duck & drake
teaching oblivious fledglings
how to play follow-the-leader.
A peace sign spreads in their wake.

Beach Time

Not even the finest Swiss watch
Could be as exact and reliable
As the girls tanning on the beach,

Turning glistening bodies with the sun,
Telling my lusting time
While their hearts tick oblivious to mine.

Soon a wolf-whistling moon will send the tide,
A red-faced sun will highdive into the sea
And our skin will turn to wrinkled hide.

Beneath the green fountain
of a palm tree
a duck loiters on one leg,
wings in white pockets.
A squirrel gallivants up
a telegraph pole,
skedaddles across the tightrope
of a humming power line.
Male crickets
improvise the same sound
with the mating call
of their wings.
They will continue
doing so until dawn.
The wings
of a young man's lopsided heart,
as he reveals his life story
to an attentive female,
transmit their own bestial,
but also celestial, mating call.
I blaze, blessed
by the brilliance of them all.

The Loudest Sound

We tightrope-walk
the shaky stepping stones
dazzled by the light
floating face up.
We settle
for the afternoon.
Finches whizz
less than an inch
above the flow,
fly-catching.
Their skittishness
is unsettling,
but as always
the water is soothing.
Downstream its gabble
is like the susurrus
of an old woman
praying to herself.
Near the fall
it's more a booming,
loud enough
to drown out
all other sound
with the loudness
of silence
pouring over,
into itself and on.

American Wake
(1995)

The Fifth Province

Meeting in a café, we shun the cliché of a pub.
　　Your sometime Jackeen accent is decaffed
like our coffee, insisting you're still a Dub.
　　You kid about being half & halfed.
The people populating your dreams are now
　　American, though the country they're set in
　　is always the Ireland within a soft Dublin.

In the country of sleep the voiceless citizens
　　trapped in my regime of dreams are Irish,
but they're all the unlikely green denizens
　　of an island that's as mysterious
as the volcano, bird or sheep islands
　　that Brendan with his homesick crew,
　　bound for the Promised Land, bumped into.

Last night I combed sleep's shore for its name.
　　A familiar adze-crowned man appeared
waving his crook's question-mark, nursing a flame
　　on a hill and impatiently declaring in weird
pidgin Irish that the fifth province is
　　not Meath or the Hy Brasil of the mind.
　　It is this island where all exiles naturally land.

After Viewing The Bowling Match at Castlemary, Cloyne, 1847

I promised to show you the bowlers
   out the Blarney Road after Sunday mass,
you were so taken with that painting
   of the snazzy, top-hatted peasant class
     all agog at the bowler in full swing,
     down to his open shirt, in trousers
as indecently tight as a baseballer's.

You would relish each fling's span
   along blackberry boreens, and delight
in a dinger of a curve throw
   as the bowl hurls out of sight,
     not to mention the earthy lingo
     & antics of gambling fans,
giving players thumbs-up or down the banks.

It's not just to witness such shenanigans
   for themselves, but to be relieved
from whatever lurks in our background,
   just as the picture's crowd is freed
     of famine & exile darkening the land,
     waiting to see where the bowl spins
off, a planet out of orbit, and who wins.

The Heritage Centre, Cobh 1993

to Catherine Coakley and Thomas McCarthy

The train might be a time machine
transporting us from the smog-shrouded city.
Chemical plants slouch down
to the Lee, flick by into the future.
We enter the simulated coffin ship,
peruse dioramas of papier-mâché emigrants
poised in various stages of travail,
accompanied by the canned clamour
of goodbyes, hooters & sailors rigging mast.

We are back doing Lent's stations
from convict ship to the grand finale
of the *Lusitania* and *Titanic,* buried
in the sea's unopened sepulchre.
The *Titanic*'s washed-up telescope
is too rusted to extend farther –
turned the wrong way around
everything diminishes and goes far off

just as our own world goes farther
each day from what we hope.
I keep doomsaying theatrics to myself,
afraid I'll sound like that filming diver
down for the first captured time in the *Titanic*,
dramatising the merest chink at every stage,
from first-class cabins below to the dark,
fathomless eternity of the gashed steerage.

The Yank

to the Irish-Irish

How were any of us wiseguy kids to know
when we mocked busloads of rotund Yanks
bleating WOW along every hedgerow
from Malin Head down to the Lee banks,
searching for the needle in the haystack
of ancestors with names like Muh-hone-ey
or Don-a-hue,
              that I'd one day come back,
a returned Yank myself, and you'd mock me
when I let slip *restroom* or *gas station.*
You accuse me of scoffing too many hot dogs,
siding unwittingly with my Vermont physician.
Now I'm even considering daily jogs,
concerned not so much for my unhealthy state,
but the scales of your eyes reading my weight.

Economic Pressure

I traipsed beneath pictures
week in week out, an urchin,
on my reluctant way upstairs
to Mr Murphy's art class.
I liked *Time Flies*, *The Falconer*,
View of Cork, *The Fiddler*,
The Bowler, *The Boxer*,
but most of all *Men of the South* –
I suppose because of the guns
and the idea of heroism
and the good & bad guys
and the 1916 anniversary
and all that hullabaloo.
I never bothered much
with that emigration canvas.
I may even have ignored it
the way I snubbed the lasher
of our class – Kathleen whatshername? –
just to show I honestly
didn't care a fig for her.
But today at the departure
gate of the airport
it caught up with me.
I saw again the woman
with her head buried
in the near shoulder
of her black-coated
son or husband.
Two men are turned away,
out of politeness,
embarrassment, or both.
One leans beneath

a scrawny tree that struggles,
like any immigrant,
in strange rock.
The other, with his back to us,
perhaps hides despair at yet
another leaving the picture.
The currach suggests
the anxiety of them all
to put the scene behind.
Its bow is aimed
away from the island's past,
out to a boat
with its sail at half mast.

Tracks of the Ancestors

to Louis de Paor

Along a boreen of bumblebees,
  blackahs & fuchsia,
somewhere around Dunquin,
  you joked that Pangaea

split there first and America
  drifted away from Kerry
and anyone standing on the crack
  got torn in two slowly.

We never dreamed we'd end up
  on other continents,
hankering for familiar mountains,
  rivers & grey firmament.

Out where you've settled,
  the aborigines
recite dreamtime songs
  that signpost journeys.

As we traverse our landscapes,
  whether city, prairie,
bush or bog, we are
  walkabout aborigine.

We can't identify where
  exactly we are from day to day,
but if we hold to songlines
  we shouldn't go astray.

Our first night here we pubcrawled
the Bronx, still too new
for us not to be enthralled
by the street life and brew

of all-night watering holes
with names like *The Shamrock*
or *Galway Shawl*, full of legals
and illegals longing to go back,

lowering pint after pint
of their staggering Irishness,
sláinte-ing the Dubs' winning point,
cursing American Guinness.

After that country for old men
abandoned them like the gannet
abandons its young,
not all of them make it.

Those that do are more
like the wren who flew high
off the eagle of folklore,
prevailing in the contentious sky.

America

I'm buffaloed
by this landscape
without voice
or memory.

Perhaps it pow-wows
with surviving Abenaki
the way Iveragh or Beara
parleys with us.

Yet I can't help but feel
I'm one of Brendan's crew,
oblivious to the nature
of the fishy shore

they settled
before the whale
beneath their feet
surged to life.

Vermont was like a wooer
whose attraction
you shut out, preoccupied
with a lifelong crush.

But lately
you've been taken
with this place,
especially since

snow covers
any resemblance
to that other one
and its perpetual row,

stilled beneath
the snow's silence.
May it snow for ever
and for ever now.

On the Renovation of Ellis Island

What is even worse than if the walls wept
like a mythical character trapped in wood
or stone is that the walls give off nothing:
nothing of all those who were chalk-branded
for a limp, bedraggled look or vacant brow;
nothing of the man who thought Liberty
wore a crown of thorns; nothing of boys
who believed that each foot of anyone
who wore pointed shoes had only one toe;
nothing of mothers clutching tattered shawls
& belt-strapped cases like Old World beliefs;
nothing of petticoated women who turned flapper.
Surely if we stripped the coats of fresh paint
as anxiously as those women undid petticoats,
walls would weep, but for nothing now, for ever.

Backfire

You recall how fireworks were invented
to ward off evil, as they rise high
above the Milky Way of Manhattan.

They form into blue, red & white stars
floating in brief constellations,
then scatter like blown dandelions.

Loudspeakers welcome back soldiers,
who plug their gas pump salutes
to their foreheads as generals cruise by.

Victory dismisses all who died.
Fireworks turn into flares for help
among the bustle & boom of bombardment.

One blossoms into a weeping willow and hangs
above skyscrapers rising like tombstones.

According to the Horticulturist, It Is Unlikely Our Fuchsia Will Survive Winter

When friends mused that literature was more
than likely kaput, our fuchsia came to mind.
Not of August's billowing plant
bought on our return from babbling Manhattan,
but of it pruned to stumpy, bare branches
in the hope of blossom next summer.
We have taken it back inside and set the pot
in the most light-enamoured window.
Regularly before bed it is watered
as the silence of snow gathers outside,
covering the stiff body of the earth.
Drops form on tips of amputated stems
in search of phantom limbs & flowers.
They could be tears for the dead, or buds.

The gold coin of the sun
slips into the slot
of a mountain gap
and up comes a full moon
that's more gold than pale.

It's as if the coin has dropped
in us and we can hear again
the music of everything.
A heron rises, clapping its wings.
A yacht nods yes.

And yes especially now
we're loafing up to Bridie's
that's more a shebeen than a pub,
loud with glorious banter
and talk about nothing.

If someone manoeuvres a singsong,
I would like to recite
something with the sway
of the seesawing sea
and the breeze massaging us

with honeysuckle, stout,
and the laughter of old friends
guffawing from the pub
to drown the thought of how
the music will play out.

Williams Was Wrong

Now I find peace in everything around me;
in the modest campion and the shoals of light
leaping across the swaying sea
and the gulls gliding out of sight.
The tops of wave-confettied rocks
slide into water and turn into seals.
They move to the lively reel
of the cove's clapping dance hall,
raising blithe yelps above the sea's music.
The ocean draws in and out like an accordion
and unseen lithe fingers play the strings
of joy on what the moment brings.
The seals close and part and close again.
Their awkward fins have turned to wings.

On the Marriage of Friends

So you have chosen the way of the swan;
the way, perhaps, that is not natural
to everyone, but I will not harp on
about heron, bluebird or dotterel,

nor how the male flycatcher pairs
with two females, keeping a mile between,
so neither cops how the other shares
the same philandering gentleman.

Did you know the life-coupling way
of the swan is also that of the crow?
And there'll be crow-black days
you'll caw at each other with blind gusto.

But there'll be times when you'll sing
the duet of the black-collared barbet,
with the first part of the song sung
by one and the second by the mate.

We wish you now many such duet days
and sing for you like the red-eyed vireo
who sings nonstop through the summer blaze
on this day you take the way of swan & crow.

While Reading Poets in their Youth

Reading by candle in the caravan
I'm disturbed by a moth fluttering
around my book and then the flame.
It drops with a waxen, burning smell
that reminds me of Icarus & Daedalus;
how I used to get the two confused
and how I've always wanted to know why
exactly moths are drawn to light;
why starlings batter themselves
at lighthouses and what safeguards
there are for those who fly by night.

Keeping Distance

The ground's still too damp,
but we find a rocky patch to
perch on. Black & white ducks
surfacedive towards us.
From the woods across
the cove a moose bellows.
A woodpecker drills
and an oriole broadcasts.
Human voices sound far off.
There is so much sweetness
in distance. The sun reflects
on the water below us.
The murkiness of the lake
after winter's sudden thaw
veils its shimmer,
turns the sun in the water
into the moon. Now I know what
the ducks are diving for –
I'll never again think Li Po,
sozzled, drowned foolishly.

Prospecting on Abbey Island

I'd like to say that the treasure hunters,
obsessively vacuuming the quiet strand
with unresponsive metal detectors,
should raise their head from the sand
and discover the treasure of the doubloon sun;
the pearl gulls hanging above the waves;
the arrow showers of mackerel on the run;
the sea surging into shimmering caves
and laying out necklace shells & starfish
on the gold carpet.
                              But now this treasure
isn't enough and I wish I didn't wish
I wanted something beyond this measure
of what normally suffices and gives peace.
What exactly I want I can't exactly say.
Perhaps it is a more permanent release
from the flotsam of trouble washed up each day.
Whatever it is seems less detectable
than finding a gold piece in sand or shingle.

At a Low Ebb

Grounded boats bask on their side
as men lean on a pint-settling counter,
having rowed in with the flood tide.

Hermit crabs retreat to their cells
of empty whelk shells over
closing black & blue mussels.

Beached, blistered bladderwrack
drapes barnacled rocks
that hide periwinkles in every crack.

Lugworm serve up spaghetti mounds of sand
as they urgently burrow for cover,
evading even the angler's hand.

Now it's time to outwit such a reach
and learn the ways of the seashore
as ebb tide's curtain lifts along the beach.

The Shrinking World

to Mary & Niall on Catherine's first summer

Reading how the European long-tailed tit
builds a perfect domed nest, gathering lichen
for camouflage, feathers to line it
and cobwebs as binding so the nest can

stretch while chicks grow, I thought of you
rushing to crying Catherine, as if her mouth shone
like those of finchlings guiding parents through
darkness. If only chainsaw-armed men,

felling whole forests by the minute,
could have seen you hover around your fledgling,
they would have immediately cut
engines and listened to your lullabying.

But their lumbering motors drone on
in the distance and perhaps approach us.
And what about all those other Catherines,
imperial woodpeckers & birds of paradise?

I sing now like the North American brown thrasher,
who at one point in its song orchestrates
four different notes: one grieves, another
frets, a third prays, but a fourth celebrates.

The Splinters

To be the conduit of tradition,
taking this familiar ink stance,
bearing the recognition
of sameness over difference.

The ferry furrows
the foam,
leaving a wake
that quickly settles
and forgets us,
as it has forgotten
all those who have
opened these waters:
fisherman, monk, pilgrim & pagan,
some foundering here.
Our mainland
world diminishes.
There is respite.
A cloud engulfs us
out of nowhere
as if the miraculous
were about to appear.
The veil lifts
to reveal the small Skellig
and Skellig Michael
rising like chapel and cathedral.

*

We forget speech, hypnotised by the climb,
concentrating on narrow, rock-hewn steps
that spiral like the gyres
of the Book of Kells, whirling in labyrinths
of knowledge, turmoil and eternity.
They lead to the beehive huts & oratories
packed with a congregation of sightseers
who whisper in disbelief and reverence
at how those sometime monks lived
in this wind-tugged cloister of shells.

We browse in each dome's live absence
and picnic above the graveyard
that's no bigger than a currach,
with a crucifix for helmsman
navigating his crew to the island of the dead.
We're eyed by the staunch, monkish puffins.
Our tongues loosen, but in keeping
with the sombreness of this sun-haloed place,
we chat about the world with an earnestness
that would embarrass us on the mainland.

You tell of how medieval monks charted world maps
with countries drawn as humans gorging upon
each other's entangled bodies. We go on to
the lands & demons of the world of poetry.
I'm flummoxed when you ask what poetry is.
I recall how the earliest musical instruments
were hewn out of bones, and that poets
carve their words out of those gone before.
They are the primitive musicians who beat
& blow words back to life. More than that I don't know.

I bask in the sun,
my head in the shade
of a rock
and doze above the ramparts
overlooking Teach Duinn.
Somehow we're ferrying
to these splintered islands once more,
tense beneath bellying canvas.
The keel parts
the seal-grey sea
and we wave to the shore.
An oneiric mist shrouds us
out of nowhere.
It vanishes as quickly.
We are here,
helping each other out
of the seesawing boat
with each uplift
of the sea's surge.
Our leaking picnic wine
turns into a libation
for the dead.
The figure of my father appears.
I reach to embrace him,
but clasp nothing.
I offer him the drink.
He waves it away, knowing
I'll need the wine
to give voice to others
who can better guide me
and that words are not necessary
between us.
His form fades

and out of his figure
another emerges
who drinks the wine
and directs the way.
Another takes his place
and another.
They drink their fill
and say their say:

Amergin
Sing of the birds' sunrise cacophony,
discordant as any orchestra
tuning up before the day's symphony.
Sing of the flocks of waves riding in,
delicately curved as a swan's neck.
Sing of the sun's descent in tongues of fire
upon the sea, communing with all and sundry.
Sing of the smell of the ocean, sweeter
than the scent of cut grass or girls;
then sing of these, for nothing is lovelier.
Sing of the broken mirror of the sea
faithful to everything passing above.
Sing of the sun pulling its own shroud over
the mirror and how shearwaters pierce the dark.
Sing of all you behold from sunrise to sunrise,
how I'm within everything wherever you go.
Who am I? Only by singing will you know.

The Old Woman of Beare
Please, do not recoil
from my shrivelled face.
Sing of how my love & I
passed our day on Skellig

long before the ebb tide
     of old age forced me
to grab the driftwood
     of God's safer love.

We slipped from the climbing,
     somnambulant pilgrimage
of bowed figures as they clasp
     their chains of beads

and edged to an outcrop
     along a narrow ledge
where kittiwakes could hardly
     reed their nest of weeds.

We clasped each other's
     trembling hands,
not so much from fear
     of being caught

by the blackbacked priest
     or falling
like wingless chicks,
     but from a need to touch.

We entwined as tightly
     as any intricate nest,
becoming our own
     nest on reaching the rock spur.

We took it as a good omen
     seeing the brace of seals
tossing the surf's lace,
     soughing as if in pain.

But if it was pain,
  it was the relief
of undressing & balming
  a fresh wound.

Our unbecoming bodies
  became our very souls
and we & the sky & the water
  swayed timelessly in time

as he surged in & out
  like the waves below
filling & emptying
  dark caves.

Edmund Spenser
  That dusk at Dún an Óir we slaughtered even
  the pregnant, whimpering women methodically
  while a bloodstained sun drowned in the ocean.
  Each foetus struggled in the belly
  of each slain mother as invisibly
  as a lobster dropped in a boiling pot.
  Had shed blood been ink, I could still be
  quilling *The Faerie Queen*, but I did not
  allow a drop to blot a mere sonnet
  that you, trapped in complicity, can never
  quite break free of. Admit it, hypocrite!
  In your time few are not guilty of slaughter.
  Even the page you'll pen this upon is of pine
  that Amazonians were shot for. I could go on.

Aodhagán Ó Rathaille

    I lifted the pitch of my grief
        above the storm-crashing waves
    for my world breaking on the reefs
        of foreign, land-grabbing knaves.

    But how can any *file* raise a plaint
        to match the world's Big House
    being undone by absentee landlords
        of Wall Street, and such dross.

    They ignore dependence upon
        the lowliest plants & creatures
    as the hermit crab & cloak anemone
        depend on one another.

    But no matter what, you must
        keen for all the world's theft
    as I keened mine, despite knowing
        that soon no one may be left.

Eoghan Rua Ó Súilleabháin

    Lend an ear to one of your own kind
        and do not let yourself be caught
    by the winds of lust, like Dante's starlings
        blown this way & that by every gust.

    I myself was borne on this wind
        as I whoremongered across the country,
    always wary that around the next bend
        some maiden would waylay me.

My rakish life squandered energy
     that I should have instilled in song
more worthy of the muse-gift given to me
     than my odd aisling.

Pay particular heed to me, especially
     since your word-talent is less than mine.
I'm still too bushed to eke out a last line.

Eibhlín Dubh Ní Chonaill
          Sing up front,
          cold-shouldering
          the fashionable
          low key of your time,
          closed, cautious & cute
          as a Kerry farmer.

          Sing as open-throated
          as my curlew-keen.
          I supped of Art's blood
          as he lay slain,
          already becoming Cork mud.

          Sing as full-throated
          as my unmatched plaint;
          matching my words
          to his cold body
          never again
          rousing to my touch.
          My hands wept
          that day's icy rain
          as I swore to undo
          that kowtowing
          dribble of a man
          who slew Art
          of the wave-white horse.

I rode the spirit of that mare
fleeter than any hare,
fleeter than any deer,
fleeter even than the wind
through Munster's open country.

Sing that elder
province of poetry.

Robin Flower

Tell of those weather-sketched
    Attic islanders
who half-tamed their school
    of rocky Blaskets,
water spouting from the blowholes
    of cliffs.

Tell how they were forced
    from their Ithaca,
still dreaming in the surf-rush
    of Irish,
perpetually longing for the lilt
    of the sea.

In them uncover the destiny
    of everyone,
for all are exiled and in search
    of a home,
as you settle the eroding
    island of each poem.

Austin Clarke

Spenser was right, but if you're trapped
    in his sonnet's complicity like someone
caught on the fourteen inaccessible steps
    mysteriously carved in the cliff
that lead neither to sea nor to higher levels,
    then fashion them with your own hammer
    in the Gaelic manner, muffling rhyme.

And since sonnets began amorous, to hell
    with the world's guilt, and tell of how such
and such a female's undulant breasts curve
    with your lust below a low-cut blouse;
how your owl-head gyroscopes on the street
    after others and how you stayed awake
    all night, illuminated in another's light.

Patrick Kavanagh

The islands' standing army
of gannets fiercely snap,
stab & peck each other
or any creature who comes near,
but none could match
the fury unleashed
on any who encroached
into my territory. I spat
abuse with petrel accuracy,
only far fouler than his spray.
I should have had the wisdom
of the sad-eyed puffins
who let everyone come close,
sensing that few mean hurt,
though when forced to tussle
they'll show their worth.

69

So learn from me,
but when I come to mind,
think not of how, brawling,
I knocked nests of words
over the edge,
splattering on the rocks
to the crude squawks of other
ravaging, wing-elbowing birds;
rather think of the winged poems
I hatched & how they're seen
regardless of time & place,
gliding & gyring
with their own certain grace.

Louis MacNeice, Dylan Thomas and other voices

Life when it is gone is like a woman
you were glad to be quit of only to find
yourself years later longing for her
when you catch her scent on a packed street.
Tell me of the seagull plundering your picnic
before it wakes you. Tell me of rain
tapping a windowpane while you're ensconced
by the fire cradling the pregnant brandy glass.
Can you still hear a distant train blow?
Wet my whistle with a slug of Guinness.
What is the texture of fresh-fallen snow?
Do girls still wear their hair in braid?
What's tea? What's the smell of the sea?
Tell me. Tell me. I am beginning to fade.

*

The alarming, silhouetted bird
has a preternatural quality
as it flutters around
my stirring head,
drawing me
from sleep's underworld,
rising with a scream.
I resist its pull.
Now everything turns
into dream's usual montage.
Another face emerges
but says nothing,
as if that's what he came to say.
His face turns into
one of a tongueless woman.
The face vanishes.
Dolphins break
beyond Blind Man's Cove,
returning the dead to Bull Island.
The ferryman's oil-wrinkled hands tug
the engine cord.
He coaxes our boat
out of the cliff-shaded cove,
opening a path
through the grape-green sea.
We withdraw
into the distance.
I wake
with the disgruntling knowledge
that we've touched only the tip
of these dark icebergs.

The Children of Lir

Today snow falls in swan-downy flakes
        reminding me of the Children of Lir,
        not solely of Fionnuala & her brothers,
        but all exiles over all the years
with only dolorous songs for company.
        The last note of their singing
        fills the air – it is the silence
        of snow slowly falling.

from *Children of Chernobyl*
(1996)

To Belarussians after Chernobyl

As I join the women on the night porch
seesawing their confab back and forth
on rockers, I think of you

or rather how I don't want to think
of what's happened to you as hurricane lamps
fan us with gentle light and gentler darkness

and the background crickets support us with
their singing wings that I can't do justice to,
nor understand, just as I can't the unknown

singing bird in the darkness of unknown trees,
nor the background soprano sopranoing,
except I've always been silently thankful

that I never understood the singer's language,
allowing the words to become wordless music.
And now more than ever I want handicapped

words to turn into such music that will recreate
a miraculous humdrum night such as ours
for you: with voices telling unbelievable tales;

with hurricane lamps, crickets, birds and trees
and one woman watering the blossoming vincas
while the other says it's best to water at night;

and how utterly I do not understand this
or anything of what shattered the glass
of your erstwhile ordinary days and nights.

The No-Go Land

It was as if we happened
    on the *Marie Celeste*,
entering a sometime home
    of a sometime town
with a table still
    laid for breakfast
and not a soul to be
    seen since the wind
blew all the arrows
    of the weathervanes
that way and invaders
    whisked everyone off.

Unmade beds hold
    the mould of sleepers
and a framed
    unknown woman cradles
a babushka-wrapped child
    and smiles into space.
An open book lies
    face down on a stand
waiting for a hand to
    turn it right side up
and children to be lulled
    again to never-never land.

Live

The photo could be of a cornfield anywhere,
but for the two forlorn, elderly gentlemen
with Tolstoy beards standing in the foreground.

The taller one to the right holds out
a loaf of bread on white linen
embroided with a crewel flower that's upside

down and hung over his unseen hands.
The man on the left is hardly taller than
what appears to be a bumper crop.

He holds a makeshift banner that could belong
to any hippie demo declaring MAKE LOVE
NOT WAR or LIVE AND LET LIVE, but I can't

decipher the black banner's Belarussian.
The white letters look jumbled, words back
to front, reminding me of what live becomes

when spelt backwards and what's hidden
behind everything these men live for now,
caught in a cornfield that could be anywhere.

Janus

The speaker elaborates on the usual statistics:
weapons, famine and so on and so earnestly forth,
to students glad to skip chemistry and physics.

They soon forget how much exam grades are worth
as the litmus paper of their hidden fear
dips beneath the surface of her facts and figures.

The crooked globe stands alone at the rear,
expelled to the dunce's corner,
declining from them into the wall.

Out of time, she assures everyone they can still
help right it all as a flock of pupils
pores over the photograph of a Chernobyl

lamb with two heads, wondering if the head
looking forward is the one living or dead.

from *The Fifth Province*
(1997)

Spiritus Hiberniae

A breeze of turf catches me out
   of the hydrangea-blue sky
as I lollygag along a boreen,
   lovely as the brine on the wind,
simplifying this island.
   It's the whiff of memory, the memory
of memory lost, reaching down
   to the deserted famine village,
breaking the hearts of ghosts
   waving handkerchiefs of whitethorn
from gaping windows across the eternity
   of the spangling Atlantic.

Film Directions for the Underworld

I recall recalling Cocteau's black and white
surreal film of a descent into the underworld
as our plane banks in early winter darkness.

We drop into rush-hour Manhattan, a volcano
spouting countless lava streams
of traffic, pouring to the outskirts over

the Styx of the East River and Hudson.
Come morning, the city will rewind
the streams back into itself.

*

To go on with this malarkey's too easy.
There's no spot more suited for some wacky movie
of a descent into a contemporary underworld

than this city. If anything
it's like the otherworld of Irish myth
whose entrance is Bull Island

off Cork and Kerry, my old homesteads.
Whatever region the souls descend to
is shrouded in perpetual mist.

*

I've a hunch the Irish underworld is the realm
of the emigrant. After exiles are waked,
they feel they've somehow passed on.

How many of those shades have disembarked
on this island after the limbo
of Ellis Island or Kennedy Airport?

They wonder, agog and aghast, how the hell
they've ended up wandering its boxed streets
without a clue, a bull's.

                    *

It's as if they're extras inside a movie, half-expecting
to see a giant gorilla swinging off the Empire State
or a star hanging by his fingertips from Liberty's torch.

They can't help feeling
that at any moment they could step out of
the film, out of the cinema and swan

Grand Parade or O'Connell Street
or Eyre Square and feel at home again, cursing
the static screen of Irish rain.

                    *

I have this shot of myself bag-slinging down
the accordion tunnel off a jet into an airport,
and though I knew no one would show up,

I still glanced round, hoping someone would be there
to welcome and guide me, or some stranger
hold my name up on a cardboard sign

like that Whitman-bearded guy held a name
printed in emerald letters. But there was no one
to meet this lone green gringo off the stagecoach.

I lugged bags through the hubbub
of hugs and cameras, overwhelmed
by the twilight zone

of the city outside,
wishing someone would press
rewind and persuade the makers

that the film doesn't
have to follow the trend where every hit
has to have the predictable unhappy end.

The Hellbox
(1998)

The Compositor

Perhaps it's the smell of printing ink
sets me off out of memory's jumbled font
or maybe it's the printer's lingo
as he relates how phrases came about.

How for instance *mind your p's & q's*
has as much to do with pints & quarts
and the printer's renown for drink
as it has with those descenders.

But I don't say anything about
how I discovered where *widows & orphans*
and *out of sorts* came from the day my father
unnoticed and unexpectedly set *30*

on the bottom of his compositor's page
and left me mystified about the origins
of that end, how to measure a line gauge
and how, since he was first to go,

he slowly and without a word
turned from himself into everyone,
as we turn into that last zero
before finally passing on to the stoneman.

The Cure

to my father

I drop into the printers and graft
to you with my hangover on hearing
the tall drinking tales of your craft
from an apprentice of yours, latching

on to the old typesetter days like myself.
He swore he could write a book.
I thought of how you were partial yourself
to a jorum or two, but you would look

down on my pint-swaggering and remind me
you kept your drinking to Saturday night,
barring births, weddings, deaths and maybe
the odd quick one if the company was right.

And for the most part I keep to that too,
but last night was a night I broke
and went on the rantan from bar to
bar, jawing with whichever bloke,

solving the world's problems drink by drink
and cigarette by cigarette, swigging
and puffing away the whole lousy stink.
You nagged away in my head about smoking

and how the butts did away with you.
But I swear the way I stood there
and yaketty-yakked, slagged and blew
smoke in the smoke-shrouded air,

coughing your smoker's cough,
I thought that you had turned into me
or I into you. I laughed your laugh
and then, knowing how you loved company,

I refused to quit the bar and leave you alone
or leave myself alone or whoever we were.
I raised my glass to your surprise return.
And now I hear you guffaw once more

as your apprentice continues to recount
printers' drink lore and asks if I know
comps at Signature O got a complimentary pint.
I joust our way out the door repeating *O O O*.

Passing the Evergreen Bar

i.m. Raymond Cunningham and Danny Delanty

Suddenly I'm back all those Saturday nights ago,
    dropping in on you as you light each other up
    and call for attention only when you call.
Your palaver is all Eagle Printing shop talk,
    fixing dancing words on the pub's correcting stone
    before the whole works is choked and broken up.
Now you set the good old days up again, and I,
    a printer's devil, pie that dumped stick,
    inserting how those times were as foul as today's.
You each take a slug, then laugh this spirit off,
    ordering me keep my moolah for the dance as you call.
I delay heading down Summerhill to the disco's strobes,
    scraps, shifts and refusals and stay for just one
more with you, forever, in the spoiled good old days.

The Composing Room

I still see those men haphazardly standing
around the comps' floor, mostly silent,
lost in their latest urgent jobs,
looking up and down as if nodding yes

from what they call their composers' sticks
as they set inverse words and lines
of each page that could be taken for
Greek scripture, declaring:

In the beginning was the Word and the Word
was made cold type and the Word was
coldness, darkness, shiny greyness
and light – and the Word dwelt amongst us.

*

Oh, I know these men would laugh this off.
They'd say, if they simply didn't throw
their eyes to heaven, that they were just ordinary
blokes trying to keep the devil from the door,

and with luck have enough left over each week
to back a few nags, and go for a few jars.
But they can't say anything or set anything now.
They are scattered from that place that's not

the same any more and many have left
any place we know of in this life,
calling to mind the old names for printing:
The Mysterious Craft or simply *The Mystery*.

I set them up in another city, another country
that's as far away in distance
from that city as it's far in time.
But they are still composing,

cracking the odd joke above
their sticks and galleys on some floor
of some building that is eternally busy
inside me even when I've forgotten

that I've forgotten them; forgetting
the world behind the word –
every time I read the word *world* I wonder
is it a typo and should I delete the *l*?

Now again I hanker to know the quality
of each letter: the weight, the texture, the smell,
the shiny new type, the ink-dark shades of old,
the different types of type, the various sizes

within the same font, the measures in ems,
picas, points and units. I'd set the words up,
making something out of all this
that stays standing – all set as masterly

as the words those men set that reveal
something of the mystery behind
and within these letters and the wonder and
the darkness, but with the lightest touch.

And the umpteen ways things can foul up
are beyond telling. Maybe the type is off,
or the typesetter may not be up
to the work, if only out of a hangover,

setting an *!* where there should be a *?*
or a *b* where there should be a *d*,
or miss aspace or a line or dingbat.
And the proofreaders don't catch the error,

passing the copy on as clean, or the make-up man
fouls the assembly page, or the stoneman errs
as he fastens the page of cold type and furniture
with the chase, turning the quoin's key.

*

Not to speak of the evil eye cast by
fellow composers who are perpetually ready
to knock the words of others, or the bosses
writing on the composition: *Kill*.

Old Shades, keep my words from such eyes
and fretting about that pied world and let me go
on regardless. And even if I foul up and the stewards
are right to set *Kill* on my last page and my words

are distributed and thrown in the hellbox,
the real achievement will be that I tried to set
the words right; that I did it with much labour
and not without a font of love. But that said,

*

grant me the skill to free the leaden words
from the words I set, undo their awkwardness,
the weight of each letter of each word
so that the words disappear, fall away

or are forgotten and what remains is the metal
of feeling and thought behind
and beyond the cast of words
dissolving in their own ink wash.

Within this solution we find ourselves,
meeting only here, through *The Mystery*,
but relieved nonetheless to meet, if only
behind the characters of one fly-boy's words.

∧

I set and reset this page,
but keep fouling each line.
It's as if the letters rage,
rebel and decline
to let any man set
down this wrong and thus
be freed himself, let
off from how typos,
word-men, typophiles,
galley-slaves, typesetters,
comps set females,
like some religious order,
in their chapel's lower case,
locking women
into a screwed chase.
This went on unseen
so long that few thought it
unjustified,
                with their obscene
wisecracks about the spirit
school for women
or about that magazine
set by women whose name I forget,
but that must be, I imagine,
the upside down peace sign or caret,
rather than the old hex
of the deleting, nameless X.

White Spirits

In the beginning, typography was denounced
as the Black Art. Though why or by whom
I can't exactly say.
                        Perhaps it had to do
with an invention's magic air, or the fear
that the spread of the word would undo souls –
it probably simply came down to printers
being eternally bedaubed in black ink.

Lately I've been thinking along the lines
of how certain compositors set words out of
their own ink-black darkness –
                                      and no matter
how strong the white spirits, they cannot
wash the ink from their hands, stained
like a weeping woman's mascara-smudged face,
or the finger-printed hands of a gangster.

Bad Impression

Right now the men put aside
    their composing sticks
and settle by the hellbox
    chatting in groups
that never seem to vary
    from day to day.
Naturally, I'm anxious to fit
    in naturally,
to be considered one amongst
    metal men and compositors.
I hesitate on the edge of
    the company, not sure
which group I should join,
    not wanting to be
solely part of any. I stroll up
    to the nearest set.
My heart pistons as fast
    as a printing machine's
and my legs are heavy
    as a case of spacers.
It's worse than approaching some
    crush on a Saturday night
to ask her for a dance
    over the disco music
that's louder than the machine floor
    in full swing.
I blurt out about
    how Cork Celtic
will kill Hibs next Sunday
    down the Box –
in the same breath I address one comp
    as the Pelé of compositors.

He slowly turns and I see myself
        inverted and fouled
in the magnifying lens of his eyes
        and in all the other eyes
turned my way, justified with his.
        He turns back, continues
what he was saying, but not
        before dumping the stick
of a wisecrack they all guffaw at.

I'm not there any more.
        I'm older than many
of those galley-slaves then.
        I walk up to the word-man
I admire and he turns
        in such a fashion.
His party laughs at his crack
        like the typesetters,
except they sip from wine glasses
        instead of chipped mugs, grasp slim
volumes and never utter a foul word.
        Nevertheless, they all turn aside
or completely away
        like mirrors turned to the wall
when someone has died.

Modern Times

for Seán Dunne

I've a notion, instead of entering the hereafter
or turning into some mythical tree,
the spirits of dead Shakers enter
the wood they fashioned with such severity.

The frigid, upright, spiny furniture
seems to withdraw as we intrude on each room
set so sparsely in this New Hampshire
ghost town that I can't imagine calling home.

And coming on the antique printer's shop
with galley pages of *The Shaker Manifesto*
locked by the quoins so no character could drop,
I long for the security of such words.

But I've lost my quoin's key
and all my shaken words fall uneven.

The Printer's Devil

to the Cork CND Office

My father led me around the composing room
and forecast comps were for the hellbox
as they set up inverse words.
He showed me how to space the space
between lines, fix leads and distribute images.

One Christmas he bought me a printer's set
like the one I use now to stamp envelopes
Compliments of this political party
or that, labouring as your apprentice to set
the upside-down, backward world aright.

But I haven't the skill to make out demons,
or the knack of stacking the characters
of politicians the right way
round and I keep smudging between the lines.

Striped Ink

I'm smack-dab in the old tabula rasa days, bamboozled
    by the books
adults bow over, musing if their eyes light upon
    the white or black spaces.

*

A boyhood later, still wren-small, on the top storey
    of The Eagle Printing Company,
I see books pour out and believe that if I fish in
    them
I'll catch   the salmon of knowledge, tall-taled
    to us at school,
out of the river of words, and like Fionn I'll
    taste
my burning hand and abracadabra I'll fathom what's
    below the surface.

*

But if I'm burnt, it's later that day, on my first
    day as pageboy, spaced from fixing leads.
The devils Fred and Dommy,
    typesetting a new book, dispatch
me down to Christy Coughlan on the box floor
    for a tin of striped ink.
I take the bait and watch floors of labouring women
    and men flit by, caught in the lift's mesh of Xs,
drowned out by the machines' hullabaloo.
    Somehow, between floors, the elevator conks out
and I'm stuck on my message that I still haven't
    cottoned on to.

Ligature

This latent mine – these unlaunch'd voices – passionate powers,
Wrath, argument, or praise, or comic leer, or prayer devout,
(Not nonpareil, brevier, bourgeois, long primer merely,)
These ocean waves arousable to fury and to death,
Or sooth'd to ease and sheeny sun and sleep,
Within the pallid slivers slumbering.

Walt Whitman, 'A Font of Type'

I trekked to the Eagle and the unassuming redbrick
        where you first set *Leaves*, forecasting how you
and all you composed in your time would be
        dismantled and distributed in the composing room
of America before being finally cast aside,
        melted down and recast in the likes of us,
each life set in its unique and sometimes fitting
        fonts and distributed or flung in
the hellbox, turning up again diffused in others.
        But it's our time to set our own lives down,
to select and fix them with our own measure
        in a ligature affixing characters who've gone
before to those close by now and way off in the future

Consider now the broken and worn types
    thrown without a word in the hellʙox of AmeriСa
      like the **BOLD**faced baglady casting
        foul woʀdꜱ at the traffic on La Guardia,
or that mackled guy holding a mackled sign
      announcing he has AIDS –– the very letteʀs
becoming their own shades — as he begs for change.

And though it's unjust to speak of anyone in terms
    of tyᴘes, if only we could design a font
   oꜰ irrᴇgulʌr ᴛypᴇ faСe made up
      of discarded images and declare it ʌ nᴇw tyᴘe.
And by setting their stories in tʜis facᴇ,
       we'd retrieve these chʌracᴛers care
lessly ᴘied with the dumping of the capitaᴟ stick.

The Lost Way

to Robert Welch

Snow was general all over Amerikay
as we Kerouaced back from Montreal
trailing our myopic headlights,
nosing through dervishing white smoke.

Miles back we took the wrong turn,
led astray by the Québecois
squabbling in their strange French at the gas station
about which way we should take.
But to give the Canucks the benefit of the doubt,
we may well have got it arseways ourselves,
given how we got lost so often that day, a parody
of Brendan or Odysseus and their mutinous crews.

*

In our rent-a-car Chevrolet Troubador
I seanchaí-ed how I ate the lotus of emigration,
never in a decade of Sundays imagining I'd be here
to stay, wincing at the word *emigrant*
that, once uttered, seems to filch me of myself
the way they say a camera steals a soul.
And there is the stranger word *immigrant*
that I've become and that my tongue that night
stuck on, the stammer itself
intimating the meaning.
                    You remarked
freeing my tongue's needle
stuck on its damaged record,
how *cúpla dán* of mine are hearkening back,

a kind of grappling for the life buoy's O
of the roads, streets and life of the drowned city
we both hail from. Outsiders,
especially those from da Pale look down
dare snotty proboscises on our corker Corkonian
dat's not just the closest ding in English to Irish,
but as nare to Elizabedan English freisin
– which is as good an excuse as any for me sonnets –
what wit our *ye* and say how we turn the word beer
into what all went down to da woods. But why *like*
is dropped into every sentence when dare's nothing
to liken the like to – ya know, like – we can't say.

*

As the windshield wipers said no to the snow
we recalled how we laboured on dismal Pre-Vatican II
Latin, Lenten nights to the men's mission, hardly out
of short pants. A partnership of visiting padres
worked on us like a pair of interrogating New York vice,
which must be, since so many of New York's finest are Micks,
where the cops learned questioning techniques.
One spotted guilt in black spots on our tongues,
condemning us to Life in Hell's Alcatraz,
setting us up for his partner
who lured us with immunity, rewards and new identities.

Then there was the hot-footed fretting along Curragh Road,
past Kiely's where we lamped the skimpy bikinied cover girl
of *Titbits* as soon as Mrs Kiely's back was turned,
and where we got the *Victor* and *Hotspur* –
I think on Fridays – after our dads doled out
our weekly pocket money of an English or Irish
threepenny bit. Which was which I could never tell.
I can still recall the forking-out, print-inked hands

of my father, setting gentle words in me, his impress,
and me swearing I'd set words like him some day.

We'd bribe cogs on undone homework mornings
with the currency of Trigger bars, lucky bags, gobstoppers,
acid drops, Hadji Beys, donkey's grudge, Taytos,
Flakes, Thompson's custard slices, liquorice snakes
black as the tongues of our souls . . . .
Though I suspect you, being brighter than *mise*, gave cogs,
and for nought, as is your nature. But how could we
out-smart-aleck the holy terrors of our childhoods?
Sister Benedict, Brother Dermot, Dantro, Leo . . . all
all too ready to root out the dodos, *amadáns*,
goms, slow ones, with endless spelling tests
and the *tuisceal ginideach* of Irish Grammar.
They turned us from our natural tongue
with their regime, more than any tallystick,
always ready with the cat-of-nine-tails of their *bataí*
while us cats perpetually ran out of nine lives.
And now the cats are out of the bag
we'll let all that catty, clergy-bashing old hat go.
Besides there were good ones too: Sister Patrick,
Brother Pius, Fabian and Brother William – who chucked it,
and according to the bible of rumour, shacked up with a nun.
And oh, John O'Shea, who could read poetry aloud
better than anyone and still can and does . . . all those
nourishing souls who blessed those hand-wringing days
and sent us on our not-so-merry, merry ways.

But I keep getting lost like our drive that day,
as if being lost is the actual right way,
taking our cue from the likes of Christy Columbus, Brendan,
Odysseus and Wrong Way Corrigan: that misdirected crew,
whose wrong ways turned out right.
Quod erat demonstrandum: the right way
being the lost way and the long way round
being the only way home, it being home.

*

All I set out to say was what has stayed with me
of that day and that drive is how I had,
corny as it sounds, a sort of epiphany:
the snowflakes scattering into the lights
were not the tatters of a torn exercise page that correcting
Brother Dermot, Sister Benedict or any of the poetry heads
tore in disgust and cast all abaa in the darkening classroom
that falling snow reminded me of earlier.
No: rather it was the inverse of the sins
of our childhood that blew over our tongues
and souls like the soot of bonfire night,
coating all the windows of our city.
The snow was manna falling,
as good a symbol as any of the nourishing company
and gab of our day, knowing with all the darkness
crowding our vision that we were blessed too
what with our families, friends and the miracle of miracles:
poetry, shagging poetry, I kid you not,
lucky enough to have come this way.

The snow fell in the silence that poetry
falls with as it drops a beneficence of
white calmness around us in the darkness.

*

The next thing I recall, as we snail-paced down
from the White Mountains was finally finding
our bearings at a crossroads with a shellityhorn-spired,
picture postcard New England church
somewhere near Morrisville that, when my friend
Chuck lived there, I nicknamed Nowheresville.

At first we thought there was something wrong,
an accident, seeing what looked like a father and son
out of their pick-up, sprawling at the roadside,
moving their arms and legs as if writhing in pain.
But then it dawned on me they were making angels,
signing their body's X signatures in a snow mound.
They might even have been aping early pioneers of flight,
Daedalus & Icarus making a myth of that myth,
finally copping that their escape plan is for the birds
and never again wanting to leave the blessèd ground.

We Will Not Play the Harp Backward Now, No

> *If in Ireland*
> *they play the harp backward at need*
>   Marianne Moore, 'Spenser's Ireland'

We, a bunch of greencard Irish,
    vamp it under the cathedral arches
    of Brooklyn Bridge that's strung like a harp.
But we'll not play
the harp backward now, harping on
       about those Micks who fashioned
this American wind lyre
and about the scores
       who landed on Ellis Island
or, like us, at Kennedy and dispersed
through this open sesame land

in different directions like the rays
    of Liberty's crown, each ray
    forming a wedge or insert symbol.
We'll refrain from inserting
how any of us craved for the old country
       and in our longing, composed a harp,
pipe, porter and colleen Tir na nOg.
And if we play
       the harp right way round now
we'll reveal another side of the story
told like the secret of Labraid the Exile: how

some, at least, found a native genius for union
    here, and where, like the Earl Gerald,
    who turned himself into a stag
and a green-eyed cat
of the mountain, many of us
        learned the trick
of turning ourselves into ourselves,
free in the *fe fiada* anonymity
            of America. Here
we could flap the horse's ears
of our singularity and not have to fear,

nor hide from the all-seeing Irish
    small town, blinking evil eyes.
    Nor does this landscape play that unheard,
but distinctly audible
mizzling slow air
        that strickens us with the plaintive notes
of the drawn-out tragedy
of the old country's sorry history.
            No, we'll not play the harp backward
any more, keeping in mind the little people's harp
and how those who hear it never live long afterward.

The Hellbox

When push comes to shove, more than anything
I didn't want to feel a foreigner
in my own, what would you call it, homeland?,
or just the *Old Country*, as here they label
anywhere across the drink and that I still,
circa a decade later, surprise myself
in casual conversation by calling *home*.
My home city, emigrating from itself, changed
so hell for leather, even if it was for the better,
that some of us felt oddly abandoned. Our one-time, dark
side streets turned into trendy shopping thoroughfares:
Paul Street, French Church Street, Half Moon Street,
Carey's Lane, where after Kojak's Nightclub
I pulled off the occasional guilt-ridden feel,
even managed the odd fumbling dry ride.
And I'll say little of how aliens like Burgerlands
and McDonald's took over main streets and buildings
in the continuous sci-fi movie of our century,
nor about the twilight zone, routing roads
that the Cork Corporation calls *da Super Highway*,
motoring over fields, woods and railway lines that still
hoot and whistle inside me down the sleepers of the years
and where we played the Easter Rising. I was
fierce Pearse, wheelchair Connolly and Cork's own Big Fella,
never Joseph *Mary* Plunkett, wearing my cowboy hat
pinned to one side Volunteer-style; though reluctantly
I took my turn at being an executing Tommy.

On other days we played Cowboys and Indians.
I was always the lone redskin brave having written
in my Santa letter one misdirected Christmas
for an Indian suit with a set of Big Chief feathers

colourful as a macaw or a bird of paradise,
spotted in Kilgrew's Toy Shop that's shot now also,
all gone Baker's John along with the aroma
of Thompson's bakery rising like dough over the Lee.
The mane of on-the-warpath feathers trailed gloriously
or flapped mid-air all those times I was hunted and fired at
as I rode Injun style, wishing there were more Indians
and I didn't all the time have to be the sole baddy
and that one of the cavalry would swap outfits
and let me be a paleface, but no one ever did.
And who else could they chase? I've this notion that
that lonesome whooping, bow and arrow Apache,
always staying one step ahead of the posse,
eventually camped way up the line in a hideout
writing his smoke-signal poems on the sky.

But I probably would have stayed put and got by
if it wasn't for some wan, some female, some cailín,
some fine half, some fla, some paragon, some Helen
of Lennox's Chipper, some Rose of Tralee, some jo,
some comely maiden, some looker, some Veronica
chucking me, ditching me, whooping me,
giving me the boot, the elbow, the old hi-di-ho.
She left me in the lurch, up the creek, up
the Swanee without a paddle, without a prayer,
pissing into the forlorn poetic gale of a wind.
Though I've a hunch I schemed the sequence of events,
so I wouldn't have to be the guilty party,
left with the dirty work of calling the shots
when the shit hits the fan of those terrible words
that were the opposite of this buckaroo's marriage proposal.
And like any true troubadour (you know that shower:
they'd shoot their grandmothers for the sake of a haiku),
I was sniffing out unrequited, gone with the wind love poems.

Yet I still muse about those happy
never after, to love, cherish and disobey days.
But what's the use? Didn't I discard all that
that morning Ger and Lou and Tom saw me off
at Dublin airport, a mite craw-sick
after my American Wake, lugging a backpack –
mostly of books – so heavy I keeled over
on my back at the arrival doors
that went on in a spasm of opening and closing,
waiting for me to pass through: harbinger
of the coming years? I lay on my back
like an insect unable to turn itself over.
And our convulsions of laughter didn't help.
I nearly wet myself. I can still see Ger
in stitches and all the passersby steering clear.
And then when the check-in lady informed me
I was over the limit, I wasn't sure if she was referring
to me or the bag that was as heavy as something in me,
though I let on nothing as I waved Hasta la vista
to my dear, high jinks, roughhousing, boozing,
poetry gun-slinging, old amigos; acting the man's man,
letting on nothing as if I was stepping on the bus
for the day down to Cobh or Youghal or Cronin's in Crosser.
And their ghosts still wave the ghost of myself
off through the mundane Cerberus of security
from that country that I was nothing more or less than,
more than less of, that's me for as long as me is.
But like Veronica, my sometime old doll,
my whilom homeland had turned strange and all wrong.

In this other country, in this other story
I yearned not for the American Irish fantasy:
the isle of jolly, stroppy drinkers; Tir na nOg;
Ballyshamrock; Innisleprechaun; the honeyed trap
of the reminiscing emigrant. But rather I hankered for

113

certain belovèd people; for the street friendliness
that I thought, before leaving entered my noggin,
was a Board Fáilte gimmick; for the landscape that as much
as it stifled us with its *dinnshenachas* of suffering,
also rooted us in a place, in an order;
not to speak of longing for the refuge
of a real pub and a proper pint of porter.
In such a state I remind myself how that island, that Thule
of another time, had given me and others short shrift,
expelling us like the Children of Lir,
not giving us the steam off its piss.

But where to? Where am I? Only an hour or so ago
that same blue-in-the-face question struck again
on sidewalks few ever walk or even rollerblade,
along the typical characterless automobile-whizzing strip
that could have been anywhere, excusing the snow,
all the way down to the handle of Miami
and across the States that get bigger and squarer
as they nudge their way to funky Califor-ni-ay;
miles of malls, hotels, motels, strip joints,
Roy Rogers, Haircuts For Less, Blockbuster Videos,
Ben Franklins, Frugal Franks, Pepper's Memphis Barbecue,
Dunkin Donuts, drive-in this, drive-in that.

I stuck my pen like a flag into this twilight zone:
an Irish Amundsen at the poetry Pole of the province
where all emigrants naturally land, except that I am Scott too,
lost and laden down with experiments,
settling into the tent that last Antarctic night
with his crew, always only a few mangy miles from home.

But to hell with all that American waking, that bull,
that myth-making crap that I probably also rigged
like the Veronica caper and mostly for the sake
of venturing to discover some new way of saying
the same old rigamarole: birth and death and everything
sandwiched between and that I have trouble fitting
my mouth around or into like one of those typical
colossal American sandwiches no one bats an eye at here.
And yes everything is larger *anseo*. Look,
even me own poems are getting blasted bigger.
I'm cross-fertilising my regular, leprechaun-small strain
with the crazy American variant, as if the Irish to-mat-o
was crossed with the whale of the Yankee to-mate-o
that itself looks like one of those radioactive mutants
of Chernobyl, along with the likes of two-headed calves
that my comrade, Adi Anti-Nuclear Roche, photographed
to show the world. Adi, save the world. Gather the ill
winds of Chernobyl into the Aeolus leather bag of your will
and blow us to the home of your dreams that are ours too,
sans thick men undoing its knot. You say there's hope still.
Outside my window chickadees jostle,
poking their mugs into the O
of the underside of our pendulum birdfeeding globe.
The seed falls from the top half of the hemisphere
of our glass like sand in an egg-timer. Already time
has run out for so many creatures, so many
now per second, so many we haven't the foggiest notion of.
Oh how can we turn the timer of the world around?
And how can poetry Adi-in and make it happen?
And Adi, even if your entreaties to make love
not war are cliché, your vision ain't. Even now
in my mind's ear I hear your gusto, revivifying
every cliché in the book. Say you're in solidarity,
in sisterhood with this. Say Maaan O Man.

Say, brother, this is the awesomeness of awesome.
Say it's not just you're in it, but we all are.
And as you mouth clichés in praise of this,
say loathsome clichés are only a way of not being alone.
Say this is cliché and I know how they love cliché, even
as cliché dulleth life. I know they've enough of aloneness.
Let us break through and come out
the other side. Let's all be together in them for once.
And oh I hereby declareth on this the tenth Day
of the tenth month in the year of Himself or Herself,
the Great Compositor, nineteen hundred and pied
ninety-five anno damini, thrown like all the other broken
and worn days into the hellbox of this century,
that *awesome* poetry should be dumped. Say I want this to be
the most laughable, spoilt job ever to be set down,
that it will be killed before it's read
and thus be the be-all and end-all truth,
since we'll all be forgotten sooner
rather than Shakespeare and even he'll eventually get dissed.
And, being the most arrogant of shams, I want the other
side of the truth of this story: how since this sublunar life
of ours is such a pain, so imperfect in one way or another,
that the more imperfect words are, the truer they are
and greater. Thus spake a Grecian saucepan.
Ergo, this clichéd pontificating litany in one fell swoop
is the greatest, awesomest piece ever written along with all
the zillions of cat-melodeon poems published in the zillions
of lousy newspapers and mags across the poetry globe,
out-McGonagalling McGonagall himself like that Canuck,
Jim McIntyre, who composed 'Ode on the Mammoth
Cheese'. The first of a langer-load of verses goeth:

> *We have seen thee, queen of cheese,*
> *Lying quietly at your ease,*
> *Gently fanned by evening breeze,*
> *Thy fair form no fly dare seize.*

Everyone laughed at him. He thought he was great. And
he was. Jimmy, old stock, you can finally rest easy.
You're the greatest. We all are. Everyone with duck-all talent
is finally coming true. We hereby decree all the crappy poets
from here to poetry's Timbuktu are greater than all
the age's Willies and Willas – and what, pray,
is *great* poetry anyway? *You gotta have heart,*
(now everyone sing along)

> *Miles and miles of heart.*
> *Oh it's nice to be a genius of course,*
> *But keep that old horse*
> *Before the cart.*

As the dark wood said to the Lion: If I were you, I'd turn
back now: *You gotta have heart,*
Miles and miles of heart.
But outside poetry's ticker, if the power of suggestion,
leaving so much to the imagination, is the chief attribute of
a poem, then Delia of the delving cleavage you're *some* poem.
Oh, when will the nine Delias descend and blow me?
O *Jesus*, there's been enough ducking and deprecating.
What about the Muses down on 42nd Street,
the ladies of my blue fantasies that come to life
in the confessional of peep-show booths,
stripping the lingerie of suggestion
slip by agonising slinky slip, dancing
into the poetry nip? Please talk dirty to me.
Sure I'm tipping. 'What's your fancy?
Titties or a hand job? Easy honey, easy.'

I could go on for ever
adding to this mumbo jumbo sandwich, but I'd better
wrap up, finish my ranting and rambling ravings.
Has everyone high-tailed it? Is there anyone there?
Was there ever any soul there? Is that snoring I hear?

All I want is not simply to parrot American voices,
    reminding me of how immigrants learned
a new tongue, mimicking gramophone records
    or following theatre stars from show to show,
pronouncing actors' lines, always a fraction behind,
    till they knew every word, so much so, according to
Ondaatje, that when Wayne Burnett dropped dead
    on stage, a Sicilian butcher in the audience took over.

I eschew such mimicry and want my words to become
    the stuff of Temelcoff's dreams – trees
changed their names and their leafy looks;
    men answered in falsetto and dogs spoke in the street.
I want to home in on the newness, strangeness, foreignness
    of everything, returning it to itself, its exile from itself,
the perpetual simultaneous goings and comings of life,
    while remaining always human, open, up front.

I'm the cocky young cleric at St Brendan's door,
    refusing to leave till I've played the music of the world:
more pleasing to me any day than the saint's dazzling angel
    who, from the altar on high, drew the bow of its beak
across the harp of its wing and played a tricksy, highbrow
    lay that was so ethereal, Brendan forever after plugged
his ears to any human harp. A pox on such angelic harping.
    Let my fingers pluck the common note of an open harp.

But who am I kidding? Where is that down-to-earth angel
    who Mossy, fellow agent of the muse, swore is sooner rather
than later going to turn up to give poetry the kiss of life
    and 'blow us all out of the water' as we mused
one night about our own strains and how the general state
    of poesy is at a low ebb. Where are you, human angel,
or whatever you are? Give us a stave, a melody, an air.
    Who are we bluffing with our efforts? Oh come on out.
We love you, Buster. Blow us all out of the water.

The Blind Stitch
(2001)

To My Mother, Eileen

I'm threading the eye
    of the needle for you again. That is
my specially appointed task, my
        gift that you gave me. Ma, watch me slip this
        camel of words through. Yes,
rich we are still even if your needlework
    has long since gone with the rag-and-bone man
        and Da never came home one day, our Dan.
    Work Work Work. Lose yourself in work.
        That's what he'd say.
            Okay okay.
Ma, listen, I can hear the sticks of our fire spit
    like corn turning into popcorn
        with the brown insides of rotten teeth. We sit
in our old Slieve Mish house. Norman is just born.
    He's in the pen.
I raise the needle to the light and lick the thread
    to stiffen the limp words. I
peer through the eye, focus, put everything out of my head.
    I shut my right eye and thread.
I'm important now, a likely lad, instead
    of the amadán at Dread School. I have the eye
        haven't I, the knack?
    I'm Prince Threader. I missed it that try.
        Concentrate. Concentrate. Enough yaketty yak.
There, there, Ma, look, here's the threaded needle back.

450 °F

to Peggy Kenneally

Peg of the swan-white hair, I'm word-stretched to give you
your due, queenmáthair of givers, never wanting more
than a quiet chat – no noodeenaw connishur –
and a cuppa Barry's cha with maybe a teaspoon or two
of sweet slagging; how you've a fella hidden somewhere;
about breaking the Pledge when Joe, the last of your lot,
your Mr Bachelor Boy son himself, knots the knot
he's tying now; how he's sure to have *your* dessert there,
your one treat: a sheer impossibility of frozen ice cream
baked in an oven turned up high enough to sap a body,
between layers of sponge cake and a frosting dream
of meringue that crumbles as quickly as would everybody
should anything happen to you. O Aunt Me Daza
this is my half-baked, dished-up effort at Baked Alaska.

A Cork Prothalamium

This is a day I'd love to sconce you in the black
    of a dressed-to-kill monkey suit
instead of the dressed-to-mourn shades of black
    we wear the odd occasion we now get to meet
    when I'm back, with muted greetings at a funeral.
But there'll be naught low key about this day of days;
    you chucking tarry-boy ways; ducking the usual
ball-and-chain crack, twigging it ain't a leaba of roses,
      but that you would be out of your tree
    to let Doris, your jag, your gauzer, your lasher,
      slip by. Joe, I'd give anything to see
you both cut a scatter up the aisle and you, the masher,
    king of ballhoppers, confetti-showered in a benevolence
      of slagging, finally getting your comeuppance.

*

Were I there, you'd be sure to razz me about that day
    you saved me from drowning in Redbarn;
you, our cozening coz, master of slagging's by-the-way,
      hop-the-ball play of affection.
But Jesus, for once I'll risk dropping the slag
    to openly say that I've great smack for you,
      how many a time you saved me from the drag
      of a dreary old Cork day – maybe bumping into
you on Blarney Street, or over a jorum – with your giddum.
So, from across the drink, this toasting prothalamium.

The gravid grey sky, languor made visible, threatens rain,
    but holds back to keep us
on edge, wind-whispering – if clouds could whisper
    what in vain we can't catch; call them
intimations of, call it the old country. But what's odd about
    this drear déjà vu is
what was once laden with melancholia, heebie-jeebies,
    willies, now seeps with comforting familiarity.

But this emigrant nostalgia run amok has far less
    to do with the drab welkin
than the concomitant grey-green water of Brookyln
    drifting into Buttermilk Channel and the waters
surrounding Ms Liberty, befouling the hem of her dress.

Like so many, I grew up in a town with a belovèd river
    the colour of slime
I took for the natural colour of all waterways. I couldn't
    fathom why teachers made us paint
the waters of our colourbooks blue, and ever since,
    passing through cities,
I hardly think twice about why I've never beheld
    a winding blue streak even on sunny days.

And as much as I'm over the moon about rumours
    of this mire's clean up
and concur with the protesters crying for the waters,
    O Aqua Mundi; as much
as I want to see the waters swell like the fish-surging
    biblical sea of the miraculous catch,
a story I loved as a kid; as much as I'd give my writing arm
    to witness trees along the banks
shake off their sickly hue, and to hear returning birds
    of the resurrected world
hosanna the airways, I admit to a silent prayer perverse.

I confess to the god of pollution in Brooklyn that if ever
    this blue, frightening to dwell on,
can be retrieved, I'll be lonesome for the iniquity of fishless
    water slouching towards the putrid shore. But heaven
on earth, I don't suppose I need worry on that score.

You'd not credit it, but tonight I lost my way and there
    wasn't a sinner to direct me
in the maze of alleys narrower than the lanes off Cork's
    norrie quays, and as manky,
when around one corner trots a funeral of Hindus
    with fanny-all on but their dhoti baydinahs.

*

I stepped aside from pallbearers shouldering
    a tinsel-covered body about the size of Kitty's,
whose bier I bore only weeks ago on the hills
    down to the ghats
of chemical factories lining the Lee, our Ganges.

I can still feel the dead weight imprinting my right
    shoulder and glimpse
taspy Joe out of badinage and a laugh, backed
    to the church wall.
We all copped another of the old world souls was cut
    from us, as Rosy was and Noel and

and and, and with each *and* a subtraction as if we're
    disappearing ourselves
limb by phantom limb. Soon we'll be nothing but air.

As the dolorous bearers wound their way, it dawned on me,
    if I followed,
they'd lead me to my lodgings above the burning ghat.
    Trailing, I felt
like an aish who tags a funeral through streets at home
    for free drink.

I doubt I could have gone farther from whatever home is
    under the embers of the Indian night
as I dekhoed a mourner scrawl the ash tilak of his dead
    before he swept the remains into
the heaven of the Ganges; the wherever of the hereafter.

*

Now monkeys lumber and loaf on the balcony outside
    my room above the cremation's glow.
I still smell of pall smoke and my eyes water as they strain
    to follow
my pencil, this jotting the leaded shade of smarting smoke
    and ashes below.

Little India

The frazzled stationmaster in his shabby excuse
for a uniform, shooing away hoi polloi, is surely
a vestige of the Raj who willed this wonder,
coupled with its compartments of class, a system
that's peanuts compared to the native one of caste,
as impossible to grasp as the rupee notes are
for the begging child with stumped hands. Leper,
the poor foreigner who throws the pittance at your feet
is too repelled to risk brushing you, even as chagrin
flushes his face. He muses how you can't even sew
for chainstores on his side of the crooked globe
and brushes such thoughts under the carpet
of his scruples. Child, it's true, I'm the stumped
angrezi who cast the sorry note and forgot you.

The Emerald Isle, Sri Lanka

The machine-gun police chat at the temple's checkpoint,
    showered by blood drops of bougainvillea,
common here as *deora dé* on our drop in the ocean.

They point out a Monitor basking in the foetor along
    the banks of Kandy's lake, where men
were once staked to its floor for speaking out.

The lizard's charcoal body is patterned with links
    as if local gods chained the creature
into itself for some accurst, centuries-old aberration.

When these oddly convivial guards tell us that magic
    words flow from the mouth of
whoever touches the lizard's tongue, I could risk prayer

at the moated temple, not for the gift of words for myself,
    but that the Tamils and
Sinhalese would risk talk, dumb and green as it sounds.

And fancying they've touched the flickering, forked tongue,
    this chevron of evil
would fan out into a spreading sign of peace.

Ululu

After the crossfire of words we lay in bed.
    I think you dropped into an obliterating sleep.
Hearing the banshee sound – a curious mixture
    of a crying cat and the keen of a loon –
I figured it was the monkey of these parts
    you told me of, trapped
and hurt, perhaps in its final throes.
    Asleep, I dreamed my body
was washed up by the ocean's procession of waves
    I'd lost myself in after our latest tempest,
and my soul had entered this creature high in the trees,
    ululating to the emptiness of the night.

The Stilt Fisherman

How glad I am
to have come to this out-of-the-way island
– ditching the hubbub of the city
with its pubs and cafés and my literati buddies –
seeking enlightenment by way of a woman.

And even if that's out of the question,
even if we can't know the world through each other,
going our separate ways, I understand why
Muslim sailors called this the Isle of Serendip
as I come upon a stilt fisherman
simply clad in a white lunghi
sitting on the perch of his stilt,
steadfast among the breakers.

*

He swings the lasso of his line
and waves me away as I swim to him,
scaring off the fish, buoyant in my stupidity.

*

Now he winds in a shimmering seerfish
and dunks it into his stilt's mesh bag.
He gives thanks and asks forgiveness of the seer.
The ocean in the swell of a wave
washes in around him.

*

I too am supplicant,
having wasted so much time,
all my life it seems,
fishing to be known.
Combers furl and fall
around him, the boom
of tall drums played in the Temple
by bowing, anonymous men.

The Malayalam Box

to Gerry Murphy and Gregory O'Donoghue

There we were, ensconced in Bewley's, that's as out of place
    in our city as I am now ferrying in a bockety boat
from Allappey to Quilon, through the razzle-dazzle
    of lagoons and lakes, in the Cork and Kerry of India.
But such oddity is nothing next to our café's confab,
    impossible to catch as the shiny spray from the prow.
Secured with the ballast of repartee, we drifted past murky
    shallow waters of literary knawvshawl and found ourselves
navigating a course I can't recall we ever traversed.
    Some shelf beneath the lagoons and canals of chat
washed away and the current carried us headlong
    immediately Gerry mentioned some artist's post-mortem:
how Seán's heart couldn't negotiate the cross-currents
    of perfection of the life and of the work.
We gave such notions the kibosh, retorting that what stopped
    our friend's, the scald's ticker
was simply the hole in the heart he was born with.

*

The boat hands chitchat among themselves in Malayalam.
    They point to where the bard Kumaran drowned
off his boat, reminding me of Tomás Rua. He lost his books
    in a ferry sinking off Derrynane, but saved himself.
We want to save ourselves also and write the *dán* of life,
    endurance and muted celebration; poetry and life
a kind of palindrome of one another like the word Malayalam.

We jawed how poesy has turned on itself, man-trapped
    like the mongoose that gnawed away at its own hind legs
to slip the trap's jaws, but whether it survives after dragging
    itself into mangroves I can't say. A boat glides by.
All-on-board wave. Why is it people on boats wave
    when, minutes later, if they passed on the street, they'd not
give each other the time of day? Maybe it's merely that we all
    navigate the same waterways along with the security
of separateness. Is that all a poem is, a wave from a boat?
    Maybe. I'm waving now from my frail, rocky craft.
Can you see me? If I pass on the street later without a nod,
    take no offence. Is that you waving from a passing raft?

*

I signal to you how I want to uncork this corker day.
    You should have seen the teal sheen of the kingfisher;
the boats, not unlike currachs, laden with copra;
    the fish owl miming stillness; the hammer & sickle flags
traipsed from huts – how they're linked to Vishnu somehow
    in my head; how every blessèd thing is somehow
threaded together; how local bards explain
    Malayalam is a box of various petals: lotus, frangipani,
cosmos; how any movement alters the words; how I shake
    these petals for you now out of my own Malayalam box.

Pathetic Fallacy

In a villa high in the hill country
I struggle to find a comfortable position
in one of those old, heavy deckchairs
with striped canvas and a real wooden frame
opening and closing out of and into itself.
It hammocks my body as the trees
sway in and out of each other
moved by what the Sinhalese waiter calls
an invisible hand of Maruti himself,
fanning the valley all the way
past Shiva's Spear and Ravana Falls,
past the squat tea bushes and the Tamil women
picking leaves for the teapots of Europe,
past lounging monkeys, past
the paddy terraces
rising in green tiers to the sky.

*

Now a woman walks against the god of the wind.
Maruti opens a space for her.
She moves away from me,
wanting to be alone,
wanting what she calls her space,
aware of my awkwardness, and her own,
away from what earlier was grace
between us, but who can stay at home
with anything for long?
Now she's just looking to be graceful
by herself. I wish her well.

*

The wind mimics the sound of falling water
in the leaves,
the sound of Ravana Falls
where the woman and I mimed the trees earlier –
the world is all intimation of sameness
defining continual difference.
The wind and trees susurrus shhhh

The Travelling Monk

The Buddhist monk in the saffron
goes all his life without a woman.
The marigold monk calls this his destiny.
At last I see, travelling by rickety train
through the deep hill country
of paddy fields and lush tea plantations
with a woman who loves me sometimes
and sometimes puts up with me gladly,
that this must be my destiny:
that I'm a holy man, a bhikku of sorts,
one of the chosen weak, one of the O so lucky.

Now quiet is everything. In your element, you sew a hem,
    satisfied you do something
as you do nothing, like myself doodling this, for once
    not angling for the great poem. A fly alights
on my left hand, then reappears, wearily checking the sand
    round my feet that's so fine it might be gold dust.
A bee must think my head, just washed in honeysuckle
    shampoo, is a flower.
The fly and the bee have fallen for me, and you too
    by the way you glance in my direction.
We're all lulled by the laid-back, jazzy soul
    singer inside our tape recorder
crooning to a woman as the palm trees
    stretch to the light,
swaying in time with the sea and your sewing hand.
    They could be the spines of local dancers.
There's ease on your brow. I say nothing. Everything
    is quiet now.

Prayer to Saint Blaise

The Buddhist monks are up chanting and pounding
    their two-sided drums.
They've been at it since before dawn across the sanctuary
    of the lake
in the Temple of the Sacred Tooth, praying to the molar
    of Buddha.
Lately I find myself mumbling a Hail Mary or Our Father
    on the quiet
as I did in the old, short pants days when I thought I was
    a goner if I missed spelling,
was late for school or confessed to impure thoughts about
    the Clark sisters, but now
I'm in trouble deep and childhood's terrors couldn't hold
    a candle to it. What matter
what the trouble is? We all know trouble – the royal
    trouble. The candle of middle age gutters down to
a malaise of disappointment about the whole hocus-pocus,
    holus-bolus ball of wax, even poesy –
I've lingered too long in the underworld of the poetry
    circle, another jostling jongleur jockeying to sup
from the blood of fame, or rather the ketchup, my ailing
    throat desperate to be heard.

*

Now I swear I'll beeline to the Holy Trinity or whatever
    chapel when I'm back in the country of churches.
I'll not care a damn if any bookish crony spots me dip
    my hand in the font
as I slip inside to kneel among the head-scarved women
    lighting votive candles,
beseeching special saints for whatever ordinary miracles.

I'll light a candle at some saint's side altar, Saint Blaise
 preferably.
Around his feast day I'll queue up for the X of a pair
 of crossed candles to wax my throat
in the hands of a priest lisping the Latin blessing
 that my voice box not fail.
Sound. I'll chance this. I'll come again to poetry pax.
 I'll kneel before my childhood's sacred tooth.

That the Brahmany Kite shares the name of a god
    is not improper
with its rufous body the tincture of Varkala's cliffs and
    white head matching the combers.
The kite riffs, banks and spirals, flapping black-tipped
    wings
mighty as the wings of the skate who might be the bird's shade
    in the stilly water.
The Brahmany makes light of the wind and circles
    the salt-and-pepper minarets of Odaayam Mosque
rising above the palms and the silence-made-susurrus
    of the Lakshadweep Sea.
Now the kite is a silhouette in the glare of the sun,
    reminding me of vultures
above the hidden Towers of Silence that Patti and I spotted
    from the Hanging Gardens.
They dined off the cadavers of followers of Zarathustra
    himself.
And, in my way, I too believe in the kasti – the sacred
    thread – of the elements
stitching us all together, and would rather the kite pluck
    the flesh from my bones
than I be laid in the dolled-up box of the West. When the time
    comes, imagine me the grub of the Brahmany.
Keep your elegy eye on the bird a day or so. Watch the kite
    make nothing of me.
Then, as I have now, give the Brahmany an almost
    imperceptible nod and turn and go.

The Greater Body

I thought the minnow was merely that turquoise flick

  but after shadowing it in
    and out of coral
I saw that the greater body
  of the creature below the dorsal fin
    is all
  but invisible most of the time, camouflaged,
flickering in & out of daily life. Look, see

The Family Man and the Rake

I'm like a character in a movie with a doppelgänger
carrying on with some looker, promising to ditch my family,
but for the kids' sake the affair must be undercover,
though he can't help parading her at the office party.
She falls for his 'you say that to all the girls' poppycock
and sometimes he falls for it too, taking a last quaff
of wine as he glances furtively at her bedside clock
before jumping in the shower to wash her scent off.
On the dash home he runs a red light and wonders
if it's an omen, slipping eternity back on his finger.
He swears, arriving once more to his dinner-in-cinders,
he was delayed at work, and breaks news of another
business trip; how the job has him too worn out to row.
You know the story. At this stage nobody can tell
the doppelgänger from the doppelgänger's doppel
in a hall of mirrors, or which one is writing this now.

The Phone Bird

For days I've stayed within range of the phone,
    tethered to my need the way the phone is tethered
        to itself. Some days I listen so hard
            I'm sure I hear it ring.
When anyone calls, they're dumbstruck
    as my shaky greeting turns to despondency.
I admit that if you rang there'd be times
    you'd get an earful for not ringing.
        You know how I brood, turned in
on myself, willing the snake-coiled phone to ring,
    the handset clamped like devouring jaws on the rest.
Now the phone's a sleeping bird with its head tucked
    back in its wing. If you call,
I'll unfurl its neck and tenderly, tenderly I'll sing.

White Worry

He mentioned his box of white noise, how
    he turns on this constant low-level static
to drown out local fighter jets on manoeuvre; the news
    channel permanently on next door; the snarl
of chainsaws devouring the sometime forest
    now become a wood, closing on our back gardens;
the siren and hooting street traffic; all the rest
    of the relentless, varying normal din.
At first, I thought how superfluous, how modern
    such contraptions are, but who am I to talk?
Look how I rely on low-level worries: the phone bill,
    a snub, something I ought to have said –
all my dear white noise switched habitually on,
    the reliable buzz in my head shrouding daily black noise.

The hummingbird
pokes its beak
into divers flowers,
all with women's names.
How right it is they should
be named after flowers, or
is it the other way round?
What time and country is it?
      You pass me the stem
          of a blossom of white wine
          and laugh and say I have
             a wandering eye for flowers
          like the hummingbird.
          But you're not annoyed.
      You know I'm loopy about women
and love even those called beautiful.
What time or country is that?
I raise my glass to you
without a word, and think
how soon I'll dip my head
between your stems
and mime the
hummingbird

148

The Bindi Mirror

The small patch which a married woman places on her forehead is known as a bindi ('zero'). These are usually bought ready-made from the market and have become almost a fashion accessory, with every imaginable shape and colour to match the occasion. You'll also come across a wide variety of used bindis stuck around the mirrors in hotel bathrooms!

India, Lonely Planet Travel Survival Kit

Here we are, ringed by the circular mirror, you in front,
    head bowed, brushing rats' nests and static
from hair that's the long, sable-silk of Indian women.
    We're oblivious of each other in that married way
that some call oneness, others call blindness. Your O
    snaps us out of our morning motions
as you spot the various bindis round our mirror.
    The index finger of your wedding-band hand traces
from one to another, connecting confetti zeros
    that are red as the razor-nick on my Adam's apple;
others are inlaid with pearls as if with love itself.
    Who wore that God's teardrop, that bloody arrowhead,
or those joyful signposts, gay-coloured as a Hindu temple?
    O women of such third eyes, did any of you grow
weary of the sold stickers on your brows, the zeros
    of your vows? While your men slept, did you vanish
into the immense Ravana dark of the Indian night?
    Could you have slipped them off like wedding rings
in hotels on our side of the faithless globe?
    Below our moving reflection are rows
of crimson bindis like tiers of shimmering votive flames.

International Call

A hand holds a receiver out a top-storey window
in a darkening city. The phone is the black,
old heavy type. From outside
what can we make of such an event?
The hand, which seems to be a woman's,
holds the phone away from her lover, refusing
to let him answer his high-powered business call.
More likely a mother has got one more
sky-high phone bill and in a tantrum warns
her phone-happy son she'll toss the contraption.
A demented widow, having cracked the number
to the afterlife, holds the receiver out
for the ghost of her lately deceased husband.
He's weary of heaven and wants to hear dusk birds,
particularly the excited choir of city starlings.
It's always dusk now, but the receiver isn't held out
to listen to the birds of the Earth from Heaven.
It's the black ear and mouth in the hand of a woman
as she asks her emigrated sisters and brothers
in a distant country if they can hear the strafing,
and those muffled thuds, how the last thud
made nothing of the hospital where they were slapped
into life. The hand withdraws. The window bangs closed.
The city is shut out. Inside now, the replaced phone
represses a moan. Its ear to the cradle
listens for something approaching from far off.

The Leper and Civil Disobedience

However, Lommán, a very arrogant leper, at the devil's instigation, was for refusing Bridget's food as usual unless Bridget gave him the spear of the aforesaid king who had gone home early that morning.... Then Saint Bridget and everybody asked him to eat but to no avail. Bridget also refused to take food until the high-handed leper ate.

Vita Prima Sanctae Brigitae

Would I were that pain in the ass, incorrigible leper
egged on, they say, by the devil, to test Saint Bridget.
She couldn't be seen to turn this sorry beggar away.
He refused a morsel. In accordance with etiquette,
no one could touch a crumb. You can imagine the curses
of diplomats, wives, officers, back-stabbers, holy men
round the hobnobbing table. Bridget, a trick up
her saint's sleeve, bade riders gallop after the king,
casting a spell that as much as the king and the army
seemed to ride, they'd not journey beyond the gates,
towing all the paraded weaponry the saint blessed earlier.
The messengers, surprised to reach the troops so soon,
related the saint's request, whereby his majesty declared:
'If Bridget were to ask for all our arms, we'd obey.'
The couriers returned, the curses hardly uttered.
Everyone tucked into piping-hot grub, cold-shouldering
Lommán as poetasters read ass-licking rhymes and fools
flattered the notables, the powers that be, with mock jokes.
All considered themselves noble for wisecracks on king,
country and themselves, laughing off vague discomfort.
As usual actors & singers elbowed each other for the limelight.
Town criers chronicled the night, who wore what and so on.
The king riding off through the night smirked to himself,
dying to test his stockpile of new model spears.

151

Bridget, playing hostess, wore a forlorn smile, avoiding
the leper's eyes, with his loathsome head in the clouds.
Lommán, feeling a clown, snickers aimed his way,
suppressed a frown, smiled at the token gesture, focused on
how many mouths the spear would feed when melted down.

Lepers' Walk

We're away for slates, secure in the gab
of our city, guffawing about spotting the talent
along the meandering, quondam river of Patrick Street.
At the disco, if the gauzer stayed past the clinger,
the fella held off till the second date and the all clear
of heavy breathing to slip the hand under a blouse
along the crepuscular Lee Fields, Lough, or Lovers' Walk
that's the epitome of a lovers' walk – the winding incline
skirts the city, bordered with necking nooks and bowers.

Having long since chucked testing such love, doing a line
now with your ersatz crush, Madam Words, you switch
to tell with a lover's ardour how Lovers' Walk
was Siúl na Lobhar in the Gaelic days, but the Sasanach,
anglicising street names, mistook the Irish v sound.
Then maybe cúpla jorums too many, feeling jilted
by our city that you can't let go, you turn inward.
You fume in a shamanistic fury about how lepers
had to steal to the contagion hospital up this hill.
They bypassed locals, themselves infected
with the typical small-town *Mycobacterium leprae*,
the paralysis that no soul dare attempt anything,
diagnosed as rising above one's station.
Whether you're right or no, for you I'd have the city
ring the bells of its malady, cleansing itself
in admission.
                    And there are other unforeseen hybrids
rampant on the islands of Academe and Literati.
We stepped onto these shores with such expectation
of goodwill and safety, certain the vaccine of learning
would immunise inhabitants from sickness, only
to find strains not unlike the small-town class: fear

of other island enclaves, numb envy
among locals, immunity to the very spirit-vaccine
they themselves dose out. How can we escape
who must be infected now too? Is there a raft,
camouflaged among palms along the patrolled banks,
that some cloudless night we can sally forth upon?
We'd raise the tattered sails of learning and be borne
on a kindly, out-of-the-dark zephyr away, guiding ourselves
by the night sky of humility, itself the journey's end.
My friend, for what else did we come all this way?

The Speakeasy Oath

to Liam Ó Muirthile

You borrowed my kimono with Japanese prints and verse
  legends of the soul's struggles,
its script more readable than the serif characters of our
  tattered Irish primers.
As you boiled water for the magic brew of Barry's tea,
  the Cork ginseng, to kick-start the day,
the kimono's druid sleeves, trailing across the stove,
  hey-presto caught fire.

Being still out for the count, I was startled awake by you
  raising the roof, ullagoning,
having a conniption, a canary, bellising 'Táim trí thine',
  'Fuck' 'Brostaigh', 'Bollox',
and a veritable string of swear words right out of the lost
  lexicon of old Irish oaths.
I vaulted out and tore into the kitchen without a stitch on.
  You were berilling
and back-berilling, in a mighty foster, like some stepdancer
  gone bonkers, lepping out a new berserk dance.

I got into the act, an bhriogáid dóiteáin, flaking the flaming
  sleeve, dousing
us pair of prancing artists with the kettle's hot water; me in
  me scald, dancing buff;
my willy, micky, connihaly, langer, crown jewels, one-eyed
  baldy man, thingamajig keeping time to the fire jig.

No sooner had we caught breath than we fell on the floor
    in stitches. A chara,
you yammered in between guffaws that it was a sign,
    a thumbs-up from the muses,
after our night before's oath to set the poetry world on fire
    while Big Joe Burrell, an fear gorm, blithely blues-sang.

Your Irish and my darned Cork-English airishin dipped
    and rose like the smoke in the yuppy Dockside,
the closest we could get to our mythical speakeasy
    with the New York mountains
across the lake leapfrogging each other into the dark
    eternity of America.

Tagging the Stealer

to David Cavanagh

So much of it I hadn't a bull's notion of
and like the usual ignoramus who casts his eyes
at, say, a Jackson Pollock or 'This Is Just to Say',
I scoffed at it. I didn't twig how it was as close
to art as art itself with its pre-game ballyhoo,
antics, rhubarbs, scheming, luck; its look
as if little or nothing is going on.
How often have we waited for the magic
in the hands of some flipper throwing a slider,
sinker, jug-handle, submarine, knuckle or screwball?
If we're lucky, the slugger hits a daisy cutter
with a choke-up or connects with a Baltimore chop
and a ball hawk catches a can of corn
with a basket catch and the ball rounds the horn.
Oh, look, Davo, how I'm sent sailing
right out of the ball park just by its lingo.
But I swear the most memorable play I witnessed
was with you on our highstools in the Daily Planet
as we slugged our Saturday night elixirs.
The Yankees were playing your Toronto Blue Jays.
They were tied at the top of the 9th.
I can't now for the life of me remember
who won, nor the name of the catcher, except
he was an unknown, yet no rookie.
Suddenly behind the pinch hitter's back he signalled
the pitcher, though no one copped until seconds later
as the catcher fireballed the potato to the first baseman,
tagging the stealer. It doesn't sound like much,
but everyone stood up round the house Ruth built
like hairs on the back of the neck, because the magic

157

was scary too. Jesus, give each of us just once
a poem the equal of that unknown man's talking hand.

The Memory Quilt

to Mona Phillips, dying

Ah, my Yankee Doodle Dandess grandma, I promised you
    this crochet of words a decade
        and a day ago. Have I, Tailor Tardy, left it too
late? Your presence here ends, to fade
    and tear. Let's call an ace a spade
        and admit, our old card-playing Baptist
    seamstress, that you're already missed,
        being here and not here, our grief patched to
your absence with that blind stitch
    you showed distaff daughter and granddaughter. Do you
        hear me? Am I dropping the stitch?
            Christ, this craft's a bitch.
Excuse me language, Mona,
    my fustian transmutations of your domestic art. Nana,
where are you off to now? Be sure to say hello
    to my Da. The first one's on me. Tell him
watch the spirits. Cheers. You'll know
    him by yours truly. Yodel an old Baptist hymn.
He likes a song. Rob too. Patti jokes that you'll find them
    two in the great smoking room of heaven.
Hobble them up a few earthly smokes from the 7-Eleven.

            *

You know, often when our home's Vermont-chilly,
    I wrap, without thinking, your quilt around me –
        the quilt with your family history
    that you outlined in the plain calico hands of Patti,
        Rob, Lois, Russell and all the other hands.
Each is stitched into the palmistry of muslin squares.

Certain life-line strands
        unravel and the hands tear.
    You wave goodbye
        from the embroidered emblems around
    yours and the other hands, the simplifying background
of each life: your sewing box, Rob's saw, Lo's threaded eye,
John's lost specs, Russ's firehat. Ah, Mona hardbye hardbye.

Heron and Li Po on the Blackwater

In an old wooden boat we motor up the Blackwater
that's now a Chinese river, what with silt-jade water,
pine and fir cliffs rising on either side, the heron
defining stillness along the banks of yellow iris,
the thatched house, two men's lightning Cork talk, and my
hangover worthy of Li Po. Even being hung over – words
that must derive from a Chinese poet's name – is a boon,
having last night burnt off rogue energy without ado.
Liam Ó and I talk poetry. We could talk poetry blue
in the face. We'll miss such gab soon enough.
At the tiller now, he negotiates shallow waters. We go
river-quiet and drift off into ourselves. I snag
in the weeds of worry and settle on how I fault Patti,
exaggerating so-called flaws in the conjugal hall of mirrors,
how say, a dress doesn't suit; how I always keep an eye
cocked for the perfect woman, Li Po's girl of Yueh, conjured
yesterday by the Yangtze Take-Away on Evergreen Street.
The heron opens its wings. I recall the story about this guy
who stumbles on a hurt heron. He nurses her well.
In gratitude, even love, she returns to him
in the guise of his dream girl of Yueh, settling
with him for good provided he stay out of her room.
Everything's hunky-dory till one day he can't resist
sneaking in, to discover the heron. On seeing his glare
accuse her that she's an illusion, the bird flies away.
It took all this time for the old story to hit home. I yak
about this or that till we row into dock. Our oars
are wings. Patti's come down to meet us. I spot her on
the leeward shore. We wave to one another.

The Blind Stitch

I can't say why rightly, but suddenly it's clear once more
    what holds us together as we sit, recumbent in the old ease
of each other's company, chewing the rag about friends,
    a poem we loved and such-like. Your Portuguese skin,
set off by a turquoise dress, doesn't hinder either.
    But there's something more than tan-deep between us.
I sew a button to a vest you made me, ravelled years ago.
    You hemmed it with the stitch you mend a frock with now.
Our hands, without thought for individual movement, sew in
    and out, entering and leaving at one and the same time.
If truth be told, the thread had frayed between us, unnoticed,
    except for the odd rip. But as we sew, love is
in the mending, and though nothing's said, we feel it
    in a lightness of mood, our ease, our blind stitch.

The Ship of Birth
(2003)

The Alien

I'm back again scrutinising the Milky Way
    of your ultrasound, scanning the dark
        matter, the nothingness, that now the heads say
    is chockablock with quarks & squarks,
gravitons & gravitini, photons & photinos. Our sprout,

who art there inside the spacecraft
    of your Ma, the time capsule of this printout,
        hurling & whirling towards us, it's all daft
    on this earth. Our alien who art in the heavens,
our Martian, our little green man, we're anxious

to make contact, to ask divers questions
    about the heavendom you hail from, to discuss
        the whole shebang of the beginning&end,
    the pre-big bang untime before you forget the why
and lie of thy first place. And, our friend,

to say Welcome, that we mean no harm, we'd die
    for you even, that we pray you're not here
        to subdue us, that we'd put away
    our ray guns, missiles, attitude and share
our world with you, little big head, if only you stay.

Paper Light

Today's light would break the hearts of the dead
      if they could step back in.
The sun filters through the lightest haze, a gauze
      of light
swabbing eye-cataracts that shroud what must be
      spirit-eyes.

It's as if the sun is seen through Japanese rice paper
      laid over
a timeless print or poem, suggesting core light
      that the sketch
or calligraphy leaves out, so the essence blazes
      through
– what the ghosts might call the divine, that may
      be seen only at one remove.

Or, as now, at one remove through this haze's tracing
      paper, the kind that as kids we simply
traced the sun, clouds, water, trees, people, cars
      and boats of our crayon-colourful world through.
As it is now and never again shall be: fawn-fall grass,
      the milkweed-seeded air, the vermilion trees,
the lake's veiled boats, the ghost of a passing truck
      and the gray scribble
on this paper white as a wimple, lit up as if from
      inside
by the unseen grand hand on this day that breaks
      the heart of a man gone all simple.

The kith and kin souls of those who've gone hover
    above the couple making love, elbow into
the woman's underworld, drinking the man's buttermilk
      in their ghostly death-drought, to recast our ilk.
Welcome Mona, olla Anna Lopes Ferreira, and you
    Rob, and all the Danny Boys. I could go on forever
invoking the dead. Each clamouring chromosome
    roll-calls out of the past, at home
      in this character small enough to set down
    within the palm of my hand. Our dust-come-to-life,
whose antique eyes have you? Whose frown?
    Whose disposition? Whose strain of strife?
We toast you now, our ancient child risen from the tomb,
kidnapped by a band of ghosts, bound in your dark room.

Morning Watch

The percolator is a gurgling alembic
    brewing the morning's spluttering slick.
I bask in the coffee's simple balm.
        For once I'll be wise and forgo
        turning to the company of the radio,
        the world's hourly news and see
        if the goldfinch and the chickadee
        will come to our feeder,
        to our coffee-brown sunflower seed.
I'll accept the responsibility of being calm.
I'll pay attention to the small creatures,
    to their broadcast and morning need.
    This morning I will pay special heed.

Sonogram

Now it's like a flashlight fanned down into the dark
      you've landed in,

not unlike a cross-section of the light wedge
revealing the missing child after the toddler
      wandered off from the picnic
      and the ground opened up
        burying him alive
        in the escape vault
     of an abandoned mine.

Each parent faulting the other.

               *

When the doctor points to a white hole,
    the screen's bright nebula,
and matter-of-factly mouths words
    we can't understand,
except for '*possible* chromosome abnormality',
    I thought of the drinking night
    about the time we gave up hitting the jackpot
    of you, our mite.
Next day I heard your mother sigh
    in the guesthouse bathroom
      as the EPT popsicle stick
      turned a stop-light red.

The doctor's words
     recalled the hangover pallor
       of her face.
They settle in her stomach like lead.

*

Our new-found mummy in a crypt,
     so fragile that even a mere gust
       must turn you to dust,
I knock on wood now for you
       in your birth box,
that we'll only have to welcome you
       into the school of normal hard knocks.

Sound Kinetics

It dawned on me as we woke to Manhattan's sea-sound
      of traffic, how this is akin to what you hear,
pressed like an ear to the shell of your mother,
      unable to match sound to moving bodies.

I could tell you, since the doctors say you can
      distinguish voices and we must converse with you,
that the scraping of a steel ladder telescoping up
      the walls outside our window, heavenward,

is secure, and that the window cleaner
      works our window into an angel's sudsy wings
before he whistles to the top storey and climbs off
      to loll away the day on cloud nine;

that the hammering is a cavil playfully
      demanding everyone on the street be quiet
to allow the sidewalk magician to saw
      a street volunteer in half; or

that the soft moans of a woman and man
      is a couple making out. These are, of course,
all hypotheses, conjectures of sound;
      tall noise without a hint

of the window cleaner's drudgery,
      the carpenter's impatience, the traffic
that is more a tinnitus than a calming susurrus,
      and, a white lie for another reason entirely,

that the moaning – which, by the way,
          has stopped now – was a couple next door
and not, of course, your Ma & Da. This is no more
          than an exposé on the kinetics of love.

Sightings

All week I've been out of kilter, down in the dumps
    for no apparent reason.
Perhaps, I've simply been too balanced, happy even,
    and the roller-coaster
god of humour, doctor Mood-Swinger himself, has said
    'Enough.
You're gettin' under my skin. Old boy, it's time for
    your general depression shot.'

*

Now it's mid-morning and I still can't get going. I potter
    round the house
and say alright, so be it, welcome Mr Down, Mr Nightday.
    old faithful companion.

*

No sooner did I shake hands with Squire Black and we get
    all chummy, inseparable even,
than this pair of goldfinch perch on either side
    of our pendulum feeder.
One's the yellowest yellow I have ever laid eyes on,
    the other's an off yellow.
They are my selves: the upbird and the off-yellow
    downbird, balancing the fulcrum. I look up.
The birds take off out of sight into the summer-thick air.
    Soon enough I'll be out of here myself.
Soon enough. That's alright now though.
    That's alright.

The Expected

You've been lying low, keeping mum
of late. On coveted nights, our chum,
your mother and I have forgotten
you're there, settling into our routine,
on the lam from quotidian strife:
money worries, the brandished knife
in the email, the hell-for-leather
workaday world, the lousy weather.
Perhaps you've sensed what lurks outside
and decided simply to hide
the way creatures do before a storm,
their antennae sensing harm.
Have you picked up how we're slow
to relinquish the world that we forgo
to have you, our sulking mouse? You see,
your mother and I are not unhappy
alone together. Do you understand?
Many a day we are grand,
simply chatting with one another,
spoofing away bother.
Chitmouse, it's impossible to explain
our lives before your reign.
It's as if we're quietly dying
and know it, wondering
at our terminal time, coveting the last
haven weeks as they trimester past.
But for your sake I'll say no more.
Mum's the word now, a stór.

Squadrons of geese fall-fly south, moving in
    and out of rank,
honking simply to stay together and to swap
    leader.
The teachers urge the children to look at fighter
    jets, the Thunderbirds,
a name taken from the great Indian bird, but
    nothing is said of that provenance.
The new god rips open the tepee vault of the sky
    above our schools and homes.
No one points out the caret of geese inserting
    themselves peacefully on the day,
or mentions what exactly the Thunderbirds
    mean to insert.
The geese unravel their chevron ranks, their echelon
    formation and, as if in civil disobedience,
reform again, but this time into a child's copybook
    correct sign.

Later tonight
it's to turn cold, the old sudden sharp
    iceberg cold of New England.
Crickets, cicadas, grasshoppers and frogs
    play on.
What their song and wing-music are saying
    I can't say,
except they must know already that the ice
    has gashed a gaping hole
in the hull of Indian Summer and they
    are the quartet
that comes out on deck and plays away
    as the great ship goes down.
We listen quietly from our deck's lifeboat.
    Play on
brave, noble souls. Play on. *Nearer, my God,*
    to thee. Nearer to thee.

Apology to Crickets

When the squadrons of night-dropped parachutists
      on D-Day were scattered far and wide
      across the occupied French countryside,
finding themselves suddenly alone in forests,
      swamps and fields swarming with the Hun,
they had these thingamajig hand crickets,
      clickers you get in Christmas stockings.
Searching in the dark to hook up with their own,
      they'd cricket-code clickclack clickclack
hearing a rustle of movement, footsteps approaching,
      waiting for the answering cricket greeting.
Tonight, little cricket, unable to hack
      news of another war, I came out to our garden
      and had nothing, nothing to cricket-call you back.

The Sea Horse Family

The sea horse is a question-mark in the ark of the ocean
     that's carried it without question all this way.
Mythical as a unicorn, and even less believable
     with its dragon head, its body a legless horse
       perpetually rearing, its monkey tail
     anchoring it to sea grass, sponge or coral,
but, my mate,
     no stranger than who you are to yourself,
     feeling large as a whale and small as a human.
Today I'd have us become sea horses, and I,
     being the male, would be the one in the family way.
I'd lug our hippocampus, our *capall mara*, our shy sea pony,
     our question-mark anchored in you,
     unquestionably unfurling its self day by tidal day.

Hero's Return

Most people are caught up in the snow-mobbed day.
    Some are even ecstatic, the snow
        is still, after all, a novelty, a show
           getting under way.
Others are already dismayed,
    cursing impassable streets, traffic delayed
      and the general disarray
of winter giving itself its own ticker tape parade.

The Shutterbug

*The day I developed the negative of a snowflake made by this method
and found it good, I felt like falling on my knees and worshipping it.*
Wilson 'Snowflake' Bentley, Jericho, Vermont, 1885

I want to be a kind of Snowflake Bentley.
After years of standing out in the below zero
weather of Jericho and neighbours declaring him
off the wall, chasing snow chimeras,
he finally caught a crystal and another and
another, invisible white flowers blooming
in the illusory snow desert of winter,
stars whose light has only just become visible,
asterisks footnoting the flaky mystery.
He recalled the Eskimo notion that snowflakes are souls
that descend and enter the expecting mother
and creep into the child's body.
                                        And now, our snowdrop,
since your body's all there and the first snow
is falling, softly falling on the world outside
our window, laying out its own carpet
maybe to welcome your soul-star, your soul-flower,
your soul-asterisk into your body
as your mother steps out on the walkway
to fetch the recycling bin. Far-fetched, right enough,
but I peer through our blind as focused
as Snowflake behind his camera's curtain,
a snatcher of snowflakes, to catch
your soulflake, the forecasted simplicity below
the whole show. I pray, as Bentley prayed
over a fresh crystal, that your flake holds,
that you're not one of those flimsy drops, but rather
a fur-flake, snug and at home as a fur-coated Eskimo
stepping out of your igloo into the universe of snow.

The Soul Hunter

The Tongans imagined the human soul to be the finer or more aeriform part of the body… something comparable to the perfume or essence of a flower as related to the more solid vegetable fiber.
  Edward Burnett Tylor, *Religion in Primitive Culture*, 1958

People have their smells too,
indefinable odours,
individual
as a fingerprint;
how I spirit-whiff
the redolence in homes
beside coffee, dinner, diaper, and other
somatic pot-pourri odour;

how a girlfriend
has a sweet scent
– a spirit balm
beyond birds' & bees' endorphin beckoners.
She forswears perfume,
costly eau de cologne,
trick-essence that wrists bedaub
to fool other spirits.

The cynic in me smells a rat, this is merely
my human need to sniff out a soul.
Still,
I'll stick to my snout,
hot on the scent of the escaped inmate,
caught from shirt or shoe,
bound to be duped again,
left staring bewildered and foolish

across the scentless bank of the widest of rivers.

181

Now the morning snowstorm is a swarm
of white locusts, not a biblical black wind
devouring all before it, but a charm
of benign creatures whose seeming simple end
is to becalm, dropping a bright humility
on the world, bringing the city to a stand-
still, turning their wings into a white sea
of, when walked on, what sounds like soft sand
that gets piled in snow combers or cotton candy,
or shaped into a button-eyed, carrot-nosed fatso.
Our plump snowman, whose eyes are still as blind
as buttons, soon we'll show you this and so
much more; how now what is called wind
blows a snow kiss, invisible as they say God is.

The Foetal Monitor Day

The Doppler is a metal detector
    combing for treasure
    that the amiable, vigilant nurse
slides over the icy hummock
of your mother's gel-rimed stomach.

*

Your pounding heart racing toward us
    is the sound of a train at full throttle,
    the tittupping of a galloping horse,
or lovers in the next room of a motel,
the headboard morse-coding against the wall.

*

Then there's the static of your grand
    kicking like someone tapping
    a mike, testing before the band
breaks into its hit song.
Our star, we're psyched to sing along.

*

The graph roll of the monitor, a tail
    curling, records the seismic shocks
    of your quakes on the foetal Richter scale,
radiating from the tectonic plate of your Da
rubbing months ago with the hypocentre of your Ma.

*

You're tucked safely as you can be
    beneath the door jamb of your small room,
    our star, train, love wave, treasure and pony.
Now you've gone quiet as a dormouse,
about to bring down your own house.

The God of Dry Mouths

A storm of tufty snow softly falling is
    white as the God placed on my child tongue,
an O or zero of white, awkward as a kiss,
    set with an Amen, as the choir sang
the Latin canticles, and head bowed,
    hands clasped, I returned to my parents' pew
in my spruce Sunday best, among a hushed loud
    litany of Amens that our God was true
and meek and simple as our set lives were,
    innocent as today's verity of perfect snow
is white. Suddenly, amid shut faces, I'm lost somewhere
    beyond the miscount of seats down to our row.
The host, cleaved to my palate, won't come unclung.
I strain to scrape the dissolving God free with my tongue.

The Present

Sparrows mostly, but chickadees,
cardinals, blue jays, wild canaries
feed all day on our bird-house stairs.
Sunflower seeds, beautiful black tears
your father gave us only a year ago.
He is dead now. How were we to know?
Snow is a white sheet laid silently upon
the body of the earth. How the dead live on.

For the Record

Today on Mallet's Bay Avenue I am undone
    by the redivivus of wonder
and not simply by the winter-blade sun
    stirring up the snow's phosphorescence, the under-
iridescence of a pigeon's neck, the jaguar
    in the guise of the svelte street cat.
                            Not simply these,
but the exhaust fuming from a passing car,
    made all the more visible by the freeze
of air, the cumulus of stacks of smoke
    billowing heavenward from McNeil's Generator
and the passing jet drawing a line of coke
    behind it on the sky's blue counter.

Yes, these are not breath or cloud or anything
    to be high on; they are undoing our skies:
the car we drive, the coffee pot plugged in each morning
    and so on and so forth, but it's nothing but lies
not to reiterate how we, the gallinaceous
    species, can fly, and make invisible flame,
and draw horseless, elephantless, assless luxurious
    cars and trucks. Give us our due all the same
and so forth and so on: how we somehow manage mostly
    to live together – confused only by ourselves, our ghostly
genes of fear and survival, too quick to be undone
    by our invention – mad simply to be under the sun.

Child, I'm reduced to playing the amateur masseur,
    quietly desperate, dropping to my knees
to tie your mother's shoes, an obedient chauffeur,
    a bag-lugging coolie eager to ease
your puffed ma as you blow her up like a balloon
    from the inside – yourself within the zeppelin,
dirigible, hot air, gas bag and rocketoon –
    without ever taking a breath, squashing
her innards, forcing her heart to faint
    on its side, her bursting bladder to leak
continually, her crushed lungs to pant
    just at a walk, her spine to bow by the week.
Soon you will become your own cone-headed arrow,
bursting your bubble, dropping into our good morrow.

The Turtle Mother

Your mother is a turtle
stranded on her back,
though with her head
– how distorted, contorted,
discombobulated you have her –
turned the wrong way round,
struggling to get up from bed
or couch, flapping her flippers,
helpless, bewildered, sad,
ancient, determined,
a stranger to herself,
and sometimes somewhat scared
hearing unseen rustlings on the banks
of choked weed, stalking, stalking.
How can a turtle know what dark
predators the day will turn up,
except they are legion? She withdraws
into her shell, your dome and home –
tucked into the thought of you?
Good shell, keep her safe and well.

Black Snow

David points at the two-day snow bunkers along Broadway,
    not the natural jaundiced yellow of melting slush,
but as if a storm of smog-snow had fallen.
    He remarks: 'That's what we breathe in every day,'
reminding me of how the nuns described the soul
    as a flake of snow and every trespass soot-darkens
that whiteness of whiteness. Ah, the soul of the world
    is made manifest to us today on Broadway and 82nd,
a fuming black exhausted snow-soul, woebegone
    as a bewildered oil-slick bird unable to fly.
I laugh, not without cynicism and apathetic stoicism, qualities
    necessary these days to survive, or rather, to get by.

The Neo-Natal

As the curtain open-sesamed on the glass chests
    of incubators – a dozen or so strewn in the cave
       of natal lights shining above resting neonate –
    I tried not to think of them as the glass-caskets
    of deceased saints or royalty and us a wave
       of mourners surging up for one last peek,
or worse again, as a kind of freak show
    as we huddled to gawk,
    though, for all the concerned talk,
somewhere a voice called 'Come up, come up, don't miss
       the smallest babies in the universe.'

They reminded me more of an aquarium
    of black molly, angel, kissing, tiger, butterfly fish
      seen in a flashy shop or restaurant
        as the winter haunts
    windows and doors with blowing ghost-veils of snow.

             *

Incubators covered with white linen
    – protecting the inhabitants from the lights' glow –
      are snug, snow-covered, gambrel-roofed homes
        in miniature, like our own right now,

    or like the shading
      laid over the canary's cage to fool the maestro
        it's night and forty winks time
  – ah, little fledglings, perk up your heads and sing.

             *

The nurse draws closed the curtain.
Each child is a magician
          immersed in a glass water tank.
After a breathtaking pause
          may the curtain be unveiled
          and each one be hailed
in a wave of relieved, silent applause.

The Coronation

Your head settles into the pelvic butterfly
    of your ma. Perhaps it's here the soul penetrates
your potentate's body as you slowly pry
    your way out of your watery, burgeoning state.
You make, at best, a willing but much-pressed
    subject and servant of your loyal queenmother,
what with your tantrums giving her small rest,
    waking her at all hours; and every other
minute ordering her to sit on the throne.
    You've grown large and despotic, a parody
of a mad medieval king who is prone
    to great and unpredictable cruelty,
and who now, if we look at Your Highness upside down,
    wears our unsettled kingdom's Pelvic Crown.

The Ship of Birth

For months your crib is docked waiting for you,
    laden with a shower of gifts:
hand-knit boots with suede soles, mounting drifts
       of rompers, bibs, hats and a slew
       of other offerings laid on your ship of birth
with the ark story embroidered all about.

In this berth the creatures have mostly mirth-
       ful faces: the cachinnating chickadees, the stout stoat,
       the grinning elephant trunk-bailing the boat,
       the droll owl, the odd rainbow trout,
       the one-humped camel you might think is pregnant
          on its back, the polar bear yodelling upon
             a melting green berg, the avuncular ant,
not to speak of the circus of unrecorded creatures on
       your kid attire. Is this saying, unbeknownst to us,
that we gather around the baby
       The Great Circus of the Earth:
          the flying hippopotamus,
          the foetal-like manatee, the dork stork,
          the delirious giraffe,
             not just for a sappy laugh,
but to illuminate their dearth
and our sapien dodo-ing as we fish-mouth sorry
sorrysorrysorrysorrysorrysorry?

Our little lambkin, waxwing, luckling,
     all the cordial choir are Noah-calling you now:
the lovelice, the leech of paradise, the how-now-down-cow,
the Forever Gone Bird, the Dolly sheep, the flying
kiwi, the crying with laughter jackass, the pronghorn,
the bristleless porcupine, the schizophrenic platypus,
       the liquorice-black crow, the rhinoceros:
         that ancestor of the unicorn
            with an overgrown thorn-horn.

Listen, the horns, the horns are blowing,
trumpeting you, our dear humacorn,
beckoning you onto the ark
     out of your first watery dark.
'Hurry now, hurry now,' baritones the polar bear.
     'Our icebergs are melting out here.'
'Quick quick,' the duck sections quack.
     'Darn, darn,'
basso-bleats the goat, stomping time with his hoof
     as the chorus raises the roof:
'All aboard, all aboard, our poor wee bairn.'

Today, noon, a young macho friendly waiter and three diners,
    business types – two males, one female –
are in a quandary about the name of the duck paddling
    Otter Creek,
the duck being brown, but too large to be a female mallard.
    They really
want to know, and I'm the human-watcher behind the nook
    of my table,
camouflaged by my stillness and nonchalant plumage.
    They really want to know.
This sighting I record in the back of my *Field Guide to People*.

The Arrival

Shades of waiting for a train in India,
    never knowing when it'll show, the dilemma
of having whiled away all curiosity in the other-
    ness of the station: the sacred cow
        humpbacked like a dromedary or your mother
back-to-front; the platform beggars who kowtow
to the foreigners as yours truly to the doctor;

the lingo, the delivery room's argot that I strain
    to make out; the fear there's no train
even as we hear your distant, unseen express
    pistoning towards us through the monsoon rain
        of monitor static and your mother's distress.
Child, even as we complain you're overdue,
we crane to catch our first glimpse of you.

A Circus

I doubt anyone would've blinked if a ringmaster
marched in among us and this blarneying broadcaster
raised a megaphone to his lips, announcing
another highlight of the Greatest Show on Earth
along with the likes of the ball-bouncing,
baby-blubber seals; the hoop-leaping lemurs of mirth;
the tremendous, stupendous fandango of horses;
highflying doctors; funambulist nurses;
and all the farraginous farrago of this Earth,
not excluding me, the whistle-blowing clown,
the huffing and puffing red-faced Bozo father
of fathers, wearing a lugubrious frown,
cracking side-splitting sideshow banter
and flat-footed jokes, a sidekick to your mother.
The whole death-defying show spun out of order
as a drum roll hailed you: the debonair,
high-flying, dare-devil god of the air,
none other than the Cannonball Kid himself
shot from the dilatory, dilative distaff
opening of your ma, the human cannon herself,
lit a little over nine months ago by your father.
Your grey jump suit was smeared with bloody gauze
as you landed in the hand-net of nurse and doctor;
the whole show agape in the pause before applause.

To My Mother

You took a deep breath. It was by what we weren't told
we were told. You sidestepped, big-talked of how cold
the winter was, how there was still a test
to come in. 'Everything will turn out for the best,
please God.' Not till your grandchild was a month old,
not wanting to spoil his entry into the fold,
did you tell us the cancer'd got you buttonholed,
casual, as if it was just a troublesome guest.
    It took your breath,
the rampant cell's stranglehold
on your alveoli, the invaded hold
of your spiritus. Your chest
tightened as the child's spirit settled in his breast.
Consoled by his arrival, you prayed it could be controlled,
    not turn out a breath for a breath.

Late Entry

The white sea of a record storm was just ploughed open;
great snow combers held back either side of the road.
There was the quality of the miraculous about the night,
a crossing over out of danger, a leavetaking
and an arrival. While your ma zipped the overnight bag,
I swabbed the breaking-waters that could've been spilt tea
on our kitchen floor. I pulled the car round to
the front, helped her in as a hooded figure scavenged
our recycle bin, our poor attempt to save the world.
I wanted to call out, say there's no need to scurry
away, a modern-day leper, but another spasm
of your overdue entry had me behind the wheel
and us off, only to be flagged down on Pearl Street
by a police road block. Two streets later a driver
in a blizzard of alcohol barred the way, refused
to allow us pass until his girlfriend implored him.
On making the hospital, the nurse assured us
you'd probably slept through it all: the groaning,
the shopping cart's leper-rattle, the swarming police
brisk in the drama of who-knows-what crime,
the drunk man's swearing and so much I've forgotten
or totally missed in the white-out of your storming.

The Language of Crying

We're still learning the language of crying,
its parent-boggling irregular grammar.
Anybody would think you were dying.

Puzzling gerunds beyond the clarifying
syllables of raw hunger's regular yammer.
We're still learning the language of crying.

Diaper-changed we take turns rock-a-bying,
bawling at each other please please be calmer.
Anybody would think you were dying:

a demented king's yowling, terrifying
soliloquy beyond a royal diaper-rash clamour.
We're still learning the language of crying.

Christ child, such a caterwaul's parent-petrifying,
hardly a put-on, you're no shammer.
Anybody would think you were dying.

Is it something you sense? A wordless prophesying?
Surely the future's not teething yet. We stammer.
We're still learning the language of crying.
Anybody would think you were dying.

Posthalamion

to a newly married couple

The snow which doth the top of Pindus strew,
Did never whiter shew . . .

Edmund Spenser, 'Prothalamion'

Today the snow takes the shape of the world,
having shimmied and trembled in the air
    all night as you slept snow-curled,
flake-furled into each other without fear
for once, of what befalls outside
    your window as if you yourself inside
made the snow fall out of inner air
confetti-ing the night in a beneficence
    of swan down, keeping souls from the graveyard,
becoming silence
made visible. And yes, you know it's hard
    on some bird or some poor soul barred outside,
    but for now you two are without a doubt
that the world in the window-shard of your yard
    is bright. The wedding-veil snow,
gossamer-light, in the shape of the shed, car, bobsleigh
and frozen lake, takes the shushed aspect of all you know.
And, looking across the whitened bay,
    you recall some deity
        laying himself down across the waterway,
allowing a brace of mortals to cross over in certain safety.

The Green Room

Shades of the green room about this scenario.
You lounge beneath the drip of the chemo,
talking shop with others, some bald, some still blest
with their own mops of hair, making the best
of your body's flaw and a visitor's melodrama.
You slip in and out of your latest part: the nausea,
dry mouth, diarrhoea, the poison's impact,
having to go back out and face the next act.
The nurse assures you that you look just fine
even in your wig, that you're eternally twenty-nine.
You perk up, introduce 'My son, the poet' to everyone.
A bald lady asks 'Do your poems rhyme like that one –
Fear no more the heat o' the sun – we did in school?
Write us one like that.' 'Okeydoke,' says I, playing the fool.

Chemotherapy

The i.v. bag hangs from the coat rack
of the stand – the revealed trick
up the sleeve
of the doctor, wizard, white-coated necromancer
who would have you believe
that this bag of what
appears to be no more than water
will save you.

Centre stage,
you sit and chat
– what can you do? –
surrounded by relatives. You're invincible as Rasputin,
forecasting the future,
feeding yourself doses of transparent poison,
outmanoeuvering your disloyal cells' rampage.

A few more treatments and you're through.
You gag.
The nurse peps
you up with banter.
She clips on a fresh drip bag
bulging above you like a strongman's flexed biceps.

Fontanelle

It wasn't until ruffling the tomentose
    of your dark hair and making a gentle tom-
        tom of your head that I felt it. My hand froze
    on the round, soft membrane of your dome.
I must have looked like doubting Thomas
    tentatively touching the unbelievable hole,
        the terrifying recess,
    withdrawing my hand from your poll,
the cerebrum beneath your skull, beneath everything,
    my eyes touch on: the cup, tea, prayer plant, book,
        trees in the window, the window, the workers painting
    across the road, the paint, the shimmering rook.
Now as your parietal bone shuts tight as a walnut,
    I excuse this as tomfoolery and myself a nut.

The Ink Moth

introducing Seamus Heaney at the Katharine Washburn
Translation Memorial

Remember our path crossed the gloaming fall path
   of *Isia Isabella*, the woolly
     bear caterpillar? You called it the furry bear.

You remarked, in between fortifying belles-lettres craic,
   how you hadn't laid eyes on one in donkey's years.
   Not since, I figured, back
     in the pupa ground of our own country.

The bog brown & black mite
– a wee concertina or bellows – traversed our drive's tarmac
     as sails beyond on the lake luffed,
   white moth wings in cuff-white wave tuft.
Someone unseen and unknown laughed,
   a lovely Lucullan disembodied laugh, breeze-lilted
     around the corner of Lake View Terrace and Berry

as Patti welcomed you, her belly a spinnaker
   swelling with the wind, the zephyr,
     of our miteling fluttering in her.

Such a luculent moment has stayed with me. You predicting
   a boy, vatic as the woolly bear
     forecasting winter.
Both of you were right, the winter being severe,
   though not for us,
  and the boy is a reality of flesh
    and bone as I coax from pupae inklings
         this ink moth.

Somewhere the woolly bear opens.
   To call it the furry bear
     is nearer eye-truth,
a miniature dowager's stole worn
to the opera, or some literary shindig. But where
   is Katharine?
She'd be in her element here.

Her company like yours, Seamus,
   was the spring touch that released in us
     the woolly bear moth,

the love moth I translate it to here,
   stuttering into the air,
   winging it here and here
                and here.

The Joker Family

You took such care of your hair.
       Now it comes out in clumps. 'Maybe
          my new grandson could spare
             a share,'
you joked, Barber Death breathing down your neck.
Always joking we are, keeping something or other in check,
       the Joker Family.

Remember how we'd beg you to open the window
       of our grey, white-topped Ford Anglia? But no,
       a mere hairline window crack of in-rushing air
         would toss your hair.
How we sweltered on those eternal drives to Everywhere:
Ringabella, Redbarn, Castlegregory, Glenbeigh.

'Now look at the scenery while the weather's fine,' you'd say,
'We'll stop soon and each have a 99,' fixing your hair
in the rear-view mirror in that special way.
Ma, any chance of a bit of air?

              *

Lately, on a drive round the Ring, near Kenmare,
       I risked wisecracking how your wig
is almost as good as your own erstwhile hair,
         itself a look-alike periwig,
and that, at least, we can open the car window.
       How we all laughed – you also.
       How the winds blow.

The West

It's a bit like the rhododendron in Kerry,
flourishing west above the lakes all the way
    to Derrynane, the wilder purple kind, beautiful
in itself, yes, beguiling, overshadowing
    quieter plants, not seeing how the shrub
winds its way around and over the native seedlings
    of ash, oak, holly, hazel, fern,
climbing their backs, suffocating them, shutting out light,
    spreading, spreading, spreading; cutting ancient links
in the great chain: the insects, birds, animals,
    even the rare deer of these parts, barring its gentle way.
Still, we're taken by this purple fantasy,
    forgetting the nightmare beneath the flower,
the monstrous root and stem-tendril arms
    that even when cut back, gain ground,
squeezing the life out of undergrowth,
    the under-strata of our shaded wood.

The Wave

I slip away
    – never being a morning person, as you say –
leaving you crisp as fresh cornflakes, playing peekaboo
       with Dan. He can't find you.
       You're putting a good face on things. Fair dues.
Even if you don't quite know the test's full news.
    I think you know.
    How can we say your body is coming undone?
Isn't everyone?

A boat is shouldered across the dunes off Lamb's Head
    like a coffin. Where do you go when you're dead?
I'd pester you about that, not much older than Danno.

Already you're making ready.
       We watch from above. Your boat bobs insecurely.
Run up the sail. Let me give you a hand. Show.
It's so clear on the horizon today
    and the water so calm beyond the bay.
    You head out beyond Bird Island towards Teach Duinn.
    A quick getaway would be a boon.
    Dan has learned to wave now too.
       He'll never remember you.
Look Ma, my hand. You'll be out of sight soon.

The Birds

At dinner a friend admired the regular birds at our feeder:
the seal-sleek grackles, the rouged house finch,
the natty chickadees, the tan mourning doves.
She asks, being a bird lover, if we'd unusual ones of late.
I mentioned the cowbirds of today. She made a face,
explained to the company how the cowbird is worse
than any Old World cuckoo, laying eggs in a wider range
of foster birds' nests, the cowfledgling killing the other brood.
As others at the table grimaced, I admitted a fondness
for the cowbird, this cowboy in the brown hood,
who, according to bird-heads, are thus since following
bison across the plains, without any time to nest.
What else could these creatures do? We survive rightly
or wrongly. And who are we to talk, us American flock?
The birds might ask – even the cowbird – who is
any person to talk? Where are the great bison herds now?
Ah, don't be so hard on the cowbirds.
They're simply caught up in old ways. And, besides,
I like their silly finch-beaks stuck on their crow heads
like those characters in that Greek comedy
about a better world, with bird beaks stuck on their pates.
Yes, like one of those characters in a Greek comedy.

The Skunk Moths

The family of skunks, their backs to me from our deck,
    are like great black & white caterpillars. I imagine them
the giant larvae of Luna moths or Monarch butterflies,
    their pupae unzipping, tremendous wings unfolding,
fluttering about the summer airways, big as people;
    each revanchist proboscis exacting retribution for those
we've not let flutter down the summers. Imagine
    their eyes, big as cow eyes, gazing, gazing at us.
Imagine the Luna's gossamer tulle wings, the tippets
    brushing us, fanning us tenderly, wrapping us in a veil,
bringing us gently to our knees in a gathering humility,
    brushing aside our mortification, finally at home, natural
in the natural world – their wings our cocoon – becoming
ourselves, pinioned resplendence, at last the human mothfly.

Aceldama

Mother

At what moment Mort entered the molecules
and triggered fanatic cells to race
ahead at the speed of night, breaking rules,
surprising the constitution,
overwhelming regular cell pace,
we'll never know; whether you were making dinner,
on the bus down town, fixing your hair,
washing dishes, up to whatever minor
essential chore you tackled with such care.
Nor can we know why Mort chose
to show up – our mother, our world, our cosmology,
our Blarney Street Gaia, our Dana – just below
the first sphere where you lugged us furled,
curled and kicking into this world.

What to do, but believe the white-coated men, Ma,
explorers of your innards, focusing a wee telescope,
on hearing of something called haematuria,
up into your system, our worldscope.

*

Pre-empt the very thought
   we have Mr Mort
           for life-long company,
the first man himself, the commander in chief we ought
   to keep in mind daily, dispatching his army,
         swarming the appalled cells one and all,
storming the good and innocent. What gall.

Our world's under general anaesethetic.
The doctor cuts the first nick.

Quick, cut out the covert platoon,
    cauterise bleeding cells,
    and not a fraction too soon.
            Are they ringing knells?
            Cut and lay them out in a bloody row,
            then suture with simple catgut. Sew
and pray to your God they don't regrow.

*

Then the suspense, the meaning of hope,
    the not-a-word-time, the learning-to-cope,
                the thinking-the-best,
the worst forgotten in these testing times, each test
    showing up okay,
    negative is the word they say.
How positive can negative be? Listen. Mort knocks.
The chap with a measured box.

*

No further symptoms,
no blood in the urine,
all your atoms
are just fine.
We should all know such days each day:
    the fridge hums,
    the kettle on the boil whistles *cha*,
    clothes on the line
    wave 'Top of the morning, Ma.'
    A shirt and a blouse link arms.
    'The drying is good today
    and not a sign
    of rain,' you say.
    The clock strikes a Saturday morning nine.

All the rooftops in our window shine,
heliographing you're fine, you're fine.

*

Brother Doctor wants to talk to us alone.
Yes, it's confirmed. It's a relapse alright.
The word *relapse* is a phone
    ringing in the middle of the night.

*

The dark cells are concealed in your bowels, head
    out undercover
        into the flow of your blood, gather
in the roots of each lung, spread,
        undo your parenchyma,
        undo the tree of your lungs, Ma.

*

I switch on the daily news to see what's old.
Mayhem and Mort are general.
It seems the whole show is terminal.
What could we do, all told?
We who have come from you.

*

Nothing else to be done, we said.
Even as we consult, the dire cells spread.
So Commander Cisplatin and Captain Taxol
    are trooped out to give that evil
        shower a taste of their own medicine,
        violence answering violence.

We stick to routine,
even joke. You ask for silence
and say, 'Now please, no fuss.
We, loves, are a credit to us.'

*

Now your spirits are up.
You request a cup
of tea – no sugar, just a drop
of milk. You sit and you sup.
You make ready again for hope,
tiresome hope.

*

Our Gaia comes apart.
Turn off the news. Have a heart.
How the world wags. Metastasis overtakes
her carcass, causing paralysis, headaches.
For earth's sakes.

All you can do now is vaguely shake your head.
The black-suited cells have nowhere else to spread.

Washing My Mother

You inclined
your chemo'd head,
a few straggly wisps of grey.
The image in the mirror,
a figure experimented on by the Schutzstaffel
of regular life, worse in a way
for being so. But we must not say so.
I sponged your neck, the bra-seared markings of your back,
soaped down the knuckles of your spine,
shut out everything,
showed not a sign.
'Is that okay?' thinking how you'd say
'I washed and powdered your bum many a day.'
No laughs now, not even to relieve awkwardness.
You answered 'Fine, love, fine.'

Nothing was stranger throughout the drear whirligig
of plans, condolences, humour-to-get-us-through
than the mortuary ringing, unsure how to fix your wig
so like your hair no one had a clue, or so we told you.
That I was your last cosmetologist played a hand
in my trembling hand. You, our cosmogony, wouldn't allow
even the meekest July zephyr ruffle a single strand,
each precious wave curling on to your brow
like the blue-tinted wavelet-furling-on-wavelet
that you paddled through on holidays in Salthill,
Silver Strand, Rossbeigh, Banna, Myrtleville
– Ma, the water wasn't near as chilly as your brow –
and you, with your hands securing your hairnet,
crying out to us in the deep: 'You'll catch cold. Come in now.'

The Hanky

You'd reach up, unpeg the clothes,
take in the great and small sails
one by one: towels, trousers,
the spinnaker shirts blowing in your face.
You worked by touch down the line
with the urgency of a sailor hauling sheets
in a storm. Out of the elements
you'd spread the tasselled ironing cloth
and lean into the pressing,
the clothes fuming under
the sizzle. There was something beyond the fury
of the perfectionist, ironing out
the last wrinkle from hankies, shirts, underpants.
Mother, did I hear you mutter again
'I'm sorry I wasn't a nun.'
'Then, Ma, where would we be?'
You pressed on, alone,
daughterless, in your kitchen cell,
the marrowfat peas softening in the pot,
the spruce spuds peeled and blind.
The brush is poised for the dust.
'Where does all the dust come from?'
 you'd quip – Ma to Ma, must
 to dust. Remember the boy offering
 to carry the pressed lot upstairs. What was it you said?
'Ah, son, I'm dead.'

*

The last time home I nicked a hanky from the ironed pile.
I'll never don it in my lapel the swanky
way you liked. Nor shake open the layered square

and let the dove flutter into the air –
how many times did you declare
you were the magician of our house?
But rather, I've a notion this handkerchief
will let fly all the cranky ills done to women
on a world you always swore was a man's;
a kind of avenging Pandora's hanky.

In Times of War

while reading W.B. Yeats and Patrick Kavanagh

So, the monocled poet delights in the two Chinamen
seated there on the cracked, lofty lapis-blue slopes
under snow drops of cherryblossom. Their serving man
caresses plaintive strings as the wise myopes
in the cute little halfway house, sipping green tea,
stare on all the tragic scene; their ancient eyes glitter gay.
Over them flies the spindly-legged bird, Longevity,
croaking in the mind's ear all will be 'Okay, Okay.'
Elsewhere, a bit along the rocky slope and of a par,
another poet eulogises geese flying in fair formation
to Inchicore, how their wings will outwing the war.
Oh, my two poets I steer by, I know my station,
but what of the mother stooped over her child,
the wild pen over the limp cygnet, the pen defiled?

US

Daily a sense of what you've become is brought home,
arrested by the sickly sweet air passing Yankee Candle
on Church Street, with its oleaginous rows,
candles made from oil, black blood of the earth.
A sense more striking as I recall walking the streets
of Paris last week. The sepia, sun-sheened buildings
turning into the gold of the oak in autumn, emitting
a kind of oxygen. I felt like one of those creatures
who breathes through its skin as I crossed St-Michel,
strolled up to the Panthéon, a city respiring with
the live dead as much as the living, a stone arboretum
giving off sustaining air. Live long in a malodorous
atmosphere and you hardly register its effluvium.

September 2003

Loosestrife

You have become your name, loosestrife,
    carried on sheep, spurting up out of ballast,
a cure brought across the deep
    to treat wounds, soothe trouble.
There have been others like you, the rhododendron,
    the cattails that you in your turn overrun.
Voices praise your magenta spread, your ability
    to propagate by seed, by stem, by root
and how you adjust to light, to soil, spreading
    your glory across the earth even as you kill
by boat, by air, by land all before you: the hardy iris,
    the rare orchids, the spawning ground of fish.
You'll overtake the earth and destroy even yourself.
    Ah, our loosestrife, purple plague, beautiful us.

Esperanto

This morning a waiter in a dingy café
    was baffled by my attempt at his language.
Everyone chimed in to translate, all strangers.
    The waiter got it, smiled
and everyone smiled. For a moment it was as if
    a great problem was solved, as if each registered
the answer we forgot we knew, the froth
    of goodwill bubbling up like cappuccino.

Opening Up

to Anthony Cronin

Yes, we're each a bit like one of those Russian figurines
    – painted in the usual garb, the figure concealing another
one within, and another within that – our actions
    often arising out of something smaller.
Say, for instance, the compliment that also spouts
    out of self-advancement; or dropping shekels in
the hat of a panhandler as the smaller self gloats
    with self-canonising charity from within
and leans on each scruple like a crutch.
    But now, aware that you're an old hand at such scrutiny
and how goodness bears its own kind of ignominy,
    I chance sending you these inklings of how much
we think of your inked life and hope you register this as a sign,
    moved by what you might dub the genuine.

Shopping for a Composter

to my mother

Rooting around what simply looked like refuse bins
I sounded out the petite clerk. Opening an exhibit,
she picked up a rotting fruit to expose worms
covering the flesh. She talked of them naturally,
endearingly even. I'll try to take a leaf from this woman
who spoke of the mass of blood-red worms as if it were a rose,
and you fresh in the grave, and I unable to help
picture you, in your coffin dark, covered with such a posy
all the way from your roman nose to your pedicured toes.

Ur God

There's something about the gourd,
how each can look so absurd,
and so different from the other – compare
the egg gourd, say, with the turk's turban
or swan with the crown of thorns, pear,
caveman's club, dolphin, pumpkin,
or the serpent inciting sin
and knowledge. How could they be kin?

They're as various as their uses:
currencies, condoms, bird-houses,
marimbas – you name it. And the name,
the concealed god within; our
gourd whispering we're all the same
beneath the rind, the god we scour
the earth for on our knees. Our word,
who art on earth, hallowed be thy gourd.

The bead-cold eyes of the Great Blue Heron,
    that should be called the Great Grey,
        spot a shiny sliver
looming beneath the water. The silverling fish
    snatches the gnats, links in the great grey chain
    – winged lightlings, gossamer light greylings.
The fish is about to forget itself
        and become the heron,
    the heron being what's called cruel and selfish too,
    but that's natural, grey-winged necessity.
The heron homes-in across the water; the water
    that's as grey as the heron, fish, rocks, day
        and the background glimmering city –
            habitat of the laughing species.
Now it's time to praise the Great Grey.

The Earth Tearer

It takes Erysichthon to get under the skin of Demeter,
axing trees of the sacred grove to construct a compound
replete with hobnobbing halls, chambers, spas, seraglio.
Even after the blade bites, bark-blood spurting upon
the earth and a green voice warns him off, he hacks on.
Though for sure, this mortal and his minions cleave limb
after limb as a way of normalising plunder
and slashing into bloody oblivion. Dryads broadcast.
Birds scatter. Animalcules and larger creatures cry.
Unseen denizens of purlieus gone for ever;
cures maybe even for Erysichthon's purblind sight.

Demeter swings into action, dispatching green heralds,
tendril pursuivants to the ends of the earth, orders Famine
to plant a hunger in him that grows the more he devours
till naught's left to procure food but to sell his own offspring –
'our legacy' he once called her. What could the child do
but shape-change, sell herself to stay with her father?
Every mouthful increases appetite till this mortal has nothing
to turn on but his body, the manducation of his own flesh,
biting into the demon of famine swelling within, his stomach
like a starving child's belly, pregnant with hunger. You can
feel the mandibles dissolve round their own dissolving flesh.

Driving in brumal, bucolic Vermont, I take a wrong
    turn, preoccupied with the radio news:
climate change, war, famine, the whole ding-dong;
    how we must choose
        as the fumes in the rear-view mirror are lowlit
           by the cold, contributing our own little bit.

The snow glistens, calling to mind the jar
    of effulgence shattering not just over
        this snowland, but over
    the chrome of a passing car,
    the farmyard's heap of manure,
even the silk-lined jackets
    of the prating Suits
    stalking the hallways
    of the Night House, hoarding the shards of light
    in underground shelters out of sight,
lying now through the din of the airways.

*

Now relax,
we must not let their dark
shroud our lightning-bug existence,
rob us of our modicum of pax,
our birthright spark,
the litscape heliographing,
the light within responding.

I locate myself again, spotting
Camel's Hump slouching
through this white country.

The seeds, shards, sparks of effulgence
shimmer over all and sundry.

Aceldama

And Judas cast down the pieces of silver in the temple, and departed.
And the priests and elders took counsel, and bought with the pieces
of silver the potter's field, to bury strangers in. Wherefore that field
has been called, The Field of Blood, unto this day.

Matthew 27:5–8

We drove down what seemed the curve
of the earth, sandwiched in our Ford Anglia.
We were happy as the colours of our beachball,
a careless car full of mirth and singalong songs,
songs that were mostly as sappy
as the soppy tomato sandwiches sprinkled with sand,
which is why they're called sandwiches our father said,
sandwiched himself now in the ground between his mother
and ours. What's the meaning of dead?
Which one of us children asked that as we passed
the spot with the lit steel cross on Carr's Hill,
putting the kibosh on the next song,
our mother about to break into *Beautiful City*?
She crossed herself, saying that's the place they bury
those whose lives somehow went wrong, betrayed
in one way or other, without a song to their names,
or a name, everyone buried together
and alone without a headstone.
The crepuscular loneliness of the field
shrouded our bright time. Our world,
the city below, shimmered like the silver pieces
scattered on the dark floor of the temple.

Notes

Notes

These annotations are mainly for non-Irish readers. For the words in Irish, a rough guide to pronunciation is included.

A number of the (often Cork) slang words and phrases recur and are annotated alphabetically here, rather than separately under each poem, with the exception of a few, notably 'The Speakeasy Oath', which has many slang words mixed up with Irish words, and 'Elegy for an Aunt'.

'Aish': a character; 'all abaa': to throw up something like sweets or a ball to be grabbed by children; 'away for slates': up and away; 'clinger': a slow dance; 'cog': to copy another student's school exercise; 'connishur': gossip; 'cut a scatter': to be well dressed; 'down the banks': criticise; 'gauzer': an attractive female; 'giddum': high spirits; 'jag': a boyfriend or girlfriend; 'jorum': a drink; 'knawvshawl': to quarrel, find fault with; 'lamp': to look at; 'lasher': an attractive female; 'manky': filthy; 'masher': a good-looking male; 'me daza': marvellous; 'noodeenaw': an annoying person; 'norrie': a northsider; 'rantan': a drinking spree; 'sconce': to look at; 'shellityhorn': a snail; 'slagging': josh; 'smack': liking; 'tarry boy': a rake; 'taspy': high spirits; 'without a bull's (notion)': without a clue.

Cast in the Fire and Southward

p.20, 'Complaint to the Watchmaker'. '*An t-am*' (un taum): the time.

p.22, 'The Rising'. *Dark Rosaleen* is an adaptation by James Clarence Mangan (1803-49) of a Gaelic aisling (ash-ling). An aisling is a traditional poem in which Ireland is depicted as a female.

American Wake

When people emigrated from Ireland to America, a get-together was held before they left. This was called an American Wake and was both festive and mournful. It was likely that the emigrant would never again see family and friends.

p.39, 'The Fifth Province'. The word for province in Irish, *cúige*, means division of five. There is still conjecture regarding the exact whereabouts of the fifth province.

p.40, 'After Viewing *The Bowling Match at Castlemary, Cloyne, 1847*'. In the game – played mostly in County Cork and County Armagh – an iron ball is thrown along a three-mile stretch of winding road. The player who covers the distance in the least throws is the winner. The painter is Daniel McDonald (1821–53). (See book cover.)

p.43, '*Economic Pressure*'. This is based on a painting of the same title by Seán Keating (1889-1977) in Crawford Municipal Art Gallery, Cork.

p.46, 'In the Land of the Eagle'. The wren became the king of the birds by flying higher than any other bird. It managed this by perching unseen on the eagle. When the eagle flew as high as it could, the wren flew off the eagle's back.

p.47, 'America'. This is one of the tales from the Hiberno-Latin narrative *Navigatio Sancti Brendani Abbatis*, which is said to have influenced Dante. Some scholars believe Brendan landed in America centuries before Columbus (who also knew the *Navigatio*).

p.48, 'Vermont Aisling'. See note to 'The Rising', p.22 above.

p.55, 'While Reading *Poets in their Youth*'. *Poets in their Youth* is a memoir by Eileen Simpson of John Berryman, Randall Jarrell, Robert Lowell and others as young poets.

p.60, 'The Splinters'. The Skelligs are almost bare rocks eight miles off the coast of County Kerry. The monastery on Skellig Michael is believed to have been founded in the sixth century. The islands are also renowned for their bird colonies. Teach Duinn is an island now known as Bull Rock, south of the Skelligs. Its name literally means 'Don's House'. Don was god of the realm of the dead. Edmund Spenser (?1552–99) was secretary to Arthur Grey, Viceroy of Ireland, when Grey ordered the massacre of more than 600 surrendered rebels at nearby Dún an Óir. Dylan Thomas (1914-53) spent a holiday in Cahersiveen and worked on a screen adaption of Muiris Ó Súilleabháin's *Fiche Blian ag Fás* (*Twenty Years a-Growing*, 1933), an autobiographical record of life on the Blasket Islands. The Blaskets, which Thomas visited, are visible just north of the Skelligs. Robin Flower (1881–1946) was an English-born scholar who lived on the Great Blasket. As well as translating literary works of the islanders, he wrote his own memoir, *The Western Island* (1945).

p.66, 'file' (fill-ih): poet.

p.67, 'aisling': see note to 'The Rising', p.22 above.

p.72, 'The Children of Lir'. Lir's three sons and one daughter were turned into swans by their stepmother and exiled from Ireland.

The Hellbox

The hellbox was a container in which worn or broken type was thrown to be melted down and recast into new type. Perhaps the most archaic words from the printer's argot, not found in dictionaries, are 'spirit' and 'fly boy', both of which are alternatives for printer's devil, or printer's apprentice. Since a significant number of printing terms have been dropped from recent editions of general dictionaries, many in *The Hellbox* are alphabetically annotated here.

'Chapel': an association of the employees in a printing office; 'composing room': the room in which the compositors set type; 'composing stick': a small metal frame much like a foot measure, within which the compositor set an individual line of type before placing it in the galley; 'demons': descenders like p and q and ascenders like b or d are called demons, as they are easy to mistake in type; 'distribute': to return types to their proper location in the cases after they have been used; 'dump the stick': to 'pie' or foul the type in the composing stick; 'dingbat': a symbol or ornament used to divide paragraphs or sections of a piece of writing; 'furniture': wooden or metal spacers that fill up larger blank areas between the set type; 'galley': a metal tray in which the compositor places lines of the typeform, thus the compositors' nickname 'galley slaves'; 'justify': to make a new line of composed type equal in width to the previous lines ; 'kill': a written instruction that the composed copy or printed matter be deleted; 'mackled': a blurred or doubled impression on a printed sheet; 'make-up man': the worker who arranged type into pages, inserting page numbers and running heads; 'pi', 'pie', or 'pied': composed type that has been spilled or spoiled; 'quoin' (pronounced 'coin'): a mechanism that locks the pages of type in a metal frame or 'chase' to be printed; 'river': a vertical streak of white space in printed matter caused by the spaces between words in several lines falling one below the other, considered to be poor typesetting; 'signature': the letter or number placed in the lower left corner of every group of pages to guide in the collating; 'sort': a letter or character that is one piece of type; 'stoneman': the printer who arranges pages of type in the correct order – the work was done on an imposing stone and called 'imposition'; 'widows and orphans': a widow is a short line ending a paragraph at the top of the page and an orphan is a sub heading or first line of a paragraph which appears alone at the foot of the page – both are considered to be inferior typesetting.

p.87, 'The Compositor'. '*30*': written to signify 'the end'.

p.101, 'Striped Ink'. See note to 'In the Land of the Eagle', p.46 above. Fionn, apprenticed to Finegas, was instructed to cook the Salmon of Knowledge after Finegas had caught it. The first person to taste it would be given complete knowledge. Fionn burnt his thumb cooking the fish and automatically put his thumb to his mouth, tasting the fish first.

p.104, 'The Lost Way'. A 'seanchaí' (shan-key) is a traditional Irish story-teller; 'cúpla dán' (coo-pla dawn): a couple of poems.

p.105, 'freisin' (fresh-in): also.

p.106, 'mise' (mis-ih): me; 'amadán' (om-ah-dawn): fool; 'tuisceal ginideach' (tui-shell gen-id-ock): the genitive case, famously difficult in Irish; 'bataí' (bot-tee): sticks or canes.

p.109, 'We Will Not Play the Harp Backwards Now, No'. The editors of the *Norton Anthology of Modern Poetry* gloss the epigraph's lines: 'The harp is the symbol of Ireland. To play it backwards is to be sentimental about the past.' 'Labraid' (Lo-er-y), an Irish king in exile, had horse's ears.
p.110, 'fe fiada' (fay fee-da): a mist or veil which renders those under it invisible.

p.111, 'The Hellbox': p.114, 'Board Fáille' (board fall-te): the Irish Tourist Board; 'dinnshenachas' (dean-shan-och-us): the topographical lore of places. 'The Children of Lir': see note to the poem 'The Children of Lir', p.72 above.
p.115, 'anseo' (un-shu): here.

The Blind Stitch

p.123, 'To My Mother, Eileen'. 'Amadán' (om-ah-dawn): fool.

p.124, '450°F'. The 'máthair' (maw-hir) of 'queenmáthair' means 'mother'.

p.125, 'A Cork Prothalamium'. 'Leaba' (lab-ah): bed.

p.128, 'Elegy for an Aunt'. A 'dhoti' is a sarong pulled up between the legs, worn by Hindu men; 'baydinah': Cork slang for a swimming costume.
p.129, 'dekhoed' derives from the Hindi word *dekho*, 'to look' and was introduced into Cork slang via soldiers serving with the British army in India; 'tilak' is a Hindu forehead marking, known as a 'tika' on a woman.

p.130, 'Little India'. 'Little India' is often applied to railway stations in India because of the teeming variety of Indian life concentrated there. The Hindi word 'angrezi' means 'foreigner'.

p.131, 'The Emerald Isle'. 'Deora dé' (joe-rah day) is the Gaelic name for fuchsia, literally meaning 'God's teardrops'.

p.135, 'The Malayalam Box'. Bewley's was a renowned set of Dublin cafés that opened franchises in other Irish cities. 'Dán' (dawn): poetry.

p.153, 'Lepers' Walk'. 'Sasanach' (soss-uh-noch): the English. The 'lobhar' of 'Siúl na Lobhar' is pronounced 'lover', but means 'leper' – the 'bh' in Irish is a v sound. 'Siúl': walk; 'cúpla' (coop-la): a couple.

p.155, 'The Speakeasy Oath'. 'Ullagoning' (ulla-go-ning): wailing; 'bellising': shouting; 'Táim trí thine' (thaw-im tree hinih): I'm on fire; 'brostaigh' (brustig): hurry; 'berilling': anti-clockwise; 'mighty foster': mighty fuss; 'lepping': leaping; 'an bhriogáid dóiteáin' (un vrig-awed toe-tawn): the fire brigade.

240

p.159, 'a chara' (ah-khara): my friend; 'fear gorm' (far gurm): 'fear' means 'man' and 'gorm' means 'blue' – black people were often called blue people in Irish; 'airishin' (arish-in): to mimick speech.

The Ship of Birth

p.174, 'The Expected'. 'A stór' is a term of endearment. It rhymes with 'more'.

p.178, 'The Sea Horse Family'. *Capall mara*: 'sea horse'.

p.206, 'The Ink Moth'. 'Craic' (crack): 'chat', 'having a good time'.

p.208, 'The Joker Family'. 'Glenbeigh' is pronounced 'Glenbay'.

p.210, 'The Wave'. 'Teach Duinn': see note to 'The Splinters', p.60 above. 'Duinn' rhymes with 'soon'.

Index of titles

Index of first lines